VICTORIOUS

LIVING

(Through the Holy Spirit)

Series: Volume 1

Victorious Living; Through the Holy Spirit
Series: Volume 1

Copyright © 2018 Reverend Dr. Kwame O. Lartey

Printed in the United States of America

Catalogued in the Library of Congress

ISBN- 13: 978-1732709225
ISBN- 10: 173270922X

Published by:
True Faith Consulting & Publishing

TABLE OF CONTENTS

ACKNOWLEDGEMENTS

This book would not have been possible without the enthusiasm of Mrs. Nana Johnson of Wichita Falls, Texas, whose husband was serving at the Air Force Base during my tenure at the church (1980-1986).

Mrs. Johnson typed endlessly and joyously on a manual typewriter to produce the first draft of this book. She learned so much as she was typing, she was an inspiration to the author. Many thanks also to Mrs. Marian McCray of East St. Louis Aldersgate United Methodist Church (1992–1997), who transcribed the typed manuscript to word processing. From there the manuscript became a book used in the Adult Sunday School Class. Mrs. McCray was also extremely excited as she completed the book.

Thanks also to Glinda Shaffer and Ron Brown who did some work for use at Hamilton Park UMC for the Prayer ministry and study on the Holy Spirit (2013).

Thanks to Ms. Romona Allen, AUMC church secretary for retyping the book for publication.

Thanks also to Rev. Archie Browne for help with editing.

Finally, thanks to Rev. Roderick Sample for assistance in the final editing of the book.

INTRODUCTION

In 1980 I was transferred from Warren UMC Charge in Terrell, Texas to Mt. Calvary UMC in Wichita Falls, Texas. The Lord had been dealing with me to study about the Holy Spirit prior to this period; but by this time the promptings of the Lord got stronger and intensified. I could never get away from the inner voice of the Spirit. But I did not want to do it. I gave all kinds of excuses why I could not do it.

The Lord would not leave me alone, though. After many years of hedging, protesting and excuses, the Lord finally got my attention. He told me to read through the New Testament and underline every verse relating to the Holy Spirit with a red ball point pen. After reading and underlining every verse, I was to start studying it. I did what the Lord told me and I was amazed. Misinformed ideas about the Holy Spirit were corrected, new insights were gained, and the Holy Spirit became a person to me. The Holy Spirit became alive, real, breathing and powerful. More than that, He became my teacher, my companion, my comforter. When my sister died suddenly, the Holy Spirit was there to comfort, strengthen, and console me. The Holy Spirit helped me deal with my grief, sorrow, and pain. The Holy Spirit is my enabler and provides the anointing for the work of God.

While serving as pastor in Wichita Falls, Texas, I started teaching people about the Holy Spirit. I gathered a group of twenty-five people or more to teach them about the Holy Spirit and to pray and intercede for the church and people everywhere. The group would gather at 10:00pm and stay past midnight. People would be so charged up, they would go to sleep at 2:00am or 3:00am, or 4:00am; they would get up by 8am and still have energy, drive, and so much joy. We had this study and prayer time on Friday nights so that people would be free to sleep in extra hours on Saturdays, if they chose. After staying in till 2:00am sometimes, nobody would be asleep by 8am Saturday morning. Good things started happening to the church in Wichita Falls, Texas. The church that had been full of turmoil and division became united; and even though we were a small congregation, a little more than a hundred people, we were a happy bunch, a family. People would visit our church and remark that they could feel the presence of the Lord, as they walked through the double doors to the sanctuary. A warm presence of love and joy would embrace them and make them want to stay or feel totally welcomed, even though they were visiting for the first time. People, who knew and visited the church before all this, would say when they are visiting "the Spirit of the Lord is here because I was here before and it did not feel this way."

During our Friday night prayers we would concentrate on people and their needs. We would spend time praying for one another. We would stay and pray for such individual or group as long as the Lord directed us to and we would try to listen and obey the Holy Spirit. Many times as we prayed in the spirit, the Lord would not allow us to stop praying until the answer was granted, or until the enemy was defeated.

The Lord taught us how to pray through until the victory is won. One night we prayed without being able to stop on our own until the Holy Spirit enabled us to pray through. When we went home, we found out why. We got a call that a nephew of a member was shot through the head with his brains oozing from his head in Dallas and left for dead. They took him to the hospital in an ambulance without any hope of his recovery, but he fully recovered. The doctors predicted that if he lived at all, he would be a vegetable but that never happened either.

The disturbing thing for me as we studied on the Holy Spirit was that, the older members in their forties and above did not want to hear about the Holy Spirit. They did not want to learn, know, or be a part of, or have anything to do with the Holy Spirit. Some even said I brought the teaching on the Holy Spirit from Africa, since it was so new to them. They thought it was evil, demonic and occultic.

During my tenure at the church at Wichita Falls, Texas, the Lord wanted me to publish my work, but I procrastinated. I thought nobody would read my work; but I promised the Lord I would do it someday. I lost my manuscript, and lamented the lost for about six years. I told the Lord that if I found the manuscript, I would not waste any more time, but would print it immediately.

Within the six-year period, I was transferred to Dallas Texas to a bigger church and with the consent of the senior pastor; we started another Friday night intercessory prayer group –from 10pm to midnight. I handpicked the group. You might say why? Because I wanted to make it available to everybody, but the Lord told me it would not work. I even went against His word, and tried it my way and it failed, so I did it the Lord's way and it worked.

Here again, I could not get anybody in their forties and above to join. The younger group in their twenties and early thirties loved it. They had a hunger for the Lord, and they came to learn and grow, and they could not believe how fast their faith grew. They were amazed that their faith could grow so fast, and so much within a few short months or even weeks.

That group prayed for miracles and healings to take place in the church; and the church which had hitherto been a "cold" traditional protestant church, started opening up. Whereas before if anyone said Amen, or raised their hands to praise God in service, people would think they were acting strangely.

Before all this, one person said to me, "What is wrong with that young man, he is always raising his hands in service" I opened to her Psalm 150 to show her that the Lord says we must praise Him with all that we have and that included lifted hands and voices.

We prayed for those who couldn't have babies. People who had been to the doctors without any help; and the Lord opened their wombs and they had beautiful babies, even twins. We prayed for God to give people a hunger and thirst for His word and Bible studies were full of eager expectant believers who were always hungry for God and His word.

Today the spiritual atmosphere of this church is far different from what it was when I arrived in 1986.

There is a prayer ministry and prayer groups at different times of the week.

In the summer of 1992 I was transferred to a small church in Illinois; and lo and behold, I found my manuscript! As you can guess, I started a Friday night intercession from 10:00pm to midnight, and a prayer vigil from 6:00am to 7:00am Monday through Friday. We started a Sunday school too, and they did not have one when I got there. I taught them about the Holy Spirit from my manuscript.

It is my prayer that as you study this book, the Lord will open your eyes and give you the spirit of wisdom and Revelation knowledge, I pray that He will enlighten your eyes so that you may know the hope of His calling, the riches of His inheritance, and the power that is made available to you as a believer; the same power that God raised Jesus from the dead with, and seated Him on His right hand and put all authorities, powers, dominions and principalities under Him, and made Him ruler over the heavens and the earth, over this world and the world to come.

I pray that through the revelation power of the Holy Spirit you will know Jesus as your Lord and Savior and confess Him as such. That you will know that God the Father Has made Jesus as head over everything for the church, which is His body and that God has placed everything under the feet of Jesus for your sake. I pray that as you study about the Holy Spirit, the fullness of God will fill you up, that you may come to know and understand God and His love in a way you have never known before and that He may do for you, and through you, more abundantly than you ever thought, imagined or asked through the mighty power of the Holy Spirit, to the glory and honor of Jesus, throughout all generations forever and ever. Amen

(See Ephesians 1:14-23; 3:14-21)

I have resisted writing my own commentary on these verses, so that the Holy Spirit Himself can teach you and give you revelation knowledge, about every verse you study. It is exciting to hear and know what the Spirit is saying to you personally, without too many biases, opinions, and doctrinal differences.

The simplicity of this book will make it appealing to all believers of varied denominational backgrounds. Anytime we can study about the Holy Spirit during this end time is extremely important. It will help us to be aware, and perceptive of what God has done, and is doing.

Billy Graham in the preface to his book on the Holy Spirit writes: "The study of the Holy Spirit is so very critical to the survival of the Church today that we must lay aside our differences and sincerely study and understand who and what the Holy Spirit is- His role in the church, in individuals, in and outside the church, and His role in the present world, and the world to come. And there is no better place to start this study than in your Bible."

Graham, Billy. *The Holy Spirit*. Waco: Word Publishing, 1978

Again, I pray that the Holy Spirit Himself will teach you and reveal these truths to you.

All scripture references are from the Good News Bible (American Bible Society Collins World 1976 unless otherwise noted).

How to Study the Holy Spirit

1. Pray the prayer of the Holy Spirit before you begin your study (See page X111). After your study pray the prayer of Grace to be Christ like (See page XV). Listen to the Holy Spirit so you may get Revelation Knowledge, Inspiration and Understanding. Psalm 119:18, 2 Timothy 3:17
2. Cross reference the particular verse you are studying, through the Old and New Testaments; with your concordance and study Bible.
3. Meditate on what you found in the Bible and through your concordance. Let God reveal to you the truth of His word. Chew on it a little more and contemplate (image, see, and intensely focus) then pray and ask God or the Holy Spirit, in the name of Jesus, to create in you or give to you what you just received by Revelation Knowledge.
4. Write what you received from God down in your notebook.
5. Study other books and commentaries on the subject and add to your knowledge of the Holy Spirit
6. As you study other books and commentaries, ask the Holy Spirit to help you discern true doctrine from false doctrine.
7. Write your final understanding of the particular verse on the Holy Spirit down. Note: If you use this for a group study be prepared for a lot of questions from your students. If you do not know or do not have the answers, do not be ashamed to say so. Tell your class however, that you will research the subject and provide them with answers for the next class
8. You may also use this study as your daily devotional or a study for your Bible class or Sunday School.
9. Prayerfully share with others, in a spirit of love, what you have learned, and you will be blessed.

THE HOLY SPIRIT PRAYER

Jesus said, "Ask and it will be given to you, Seek and you will find, Knock and it will be opened to you. For everyone who asks receives, and he who seeks finds and to him who knocks, it will be opened".
Matthew 7:7,8 (NKJV)

"On the last day, the great day of the feast, Jesus stood and cried out, saying, 'If anyone thirsts, let him come to Me and drink. He who believes in Me, as the Scripture has said, out of his heart will flow rivers of living water'. But He spoke this concerning the Spirit, whom, those believing in Him would receive; for the Holy Spirit was not yet given, because Jesus was not yet glorified." John 7:37-39 (NKJV)

Prayer to the Holy Spirit

*O God the Holy Spirit,
(Romans 8:8-11)
Come to me and dwell in me.
(Ephesians 1:13,14)
Come as the wind and recreate and cleanse me. (Psalm 19:12; John 3:5-8)
Come as the anointing of God and fill me with power for good works. (Ephesians 2:10)
Come as the fire and burn all the garbage and dross in me.
(Acts 2:1-4)
Come as the dew and refresh me. (Genesis 27:22)
Come as the rain and wash and purify me. (Psalm 51:1-5)
Come as the balm of Gilead and heal my wounds, pains, regrets, and sorrows. (Jeremiah 8:21,22)
Come as the breeze and ease my fears, doubts, worries, and anxieties. (Philippians 4:4-6)

Come as the Counselor and Comforter and counsel and comfort me. Come as the Teacher and teach me. (John 14:15-21)
Come as the Physician and Healer and heal all my sicknesses and diseases. (Exodus 15:26)
Come as the Power of God and empower me to take authority over all the powers of the enemy so that nothing shall by no means hurt me. (Luke 10:19)
*O Great Spirit, Holy Spirit.
(Romans 8:8-16)
Whose breath gives life to the dead. (John 11:25)
And whose voice is heard in the soft breeze, I need Your strength and Your wisdom. (Proverbs 8; Revelations 5:12)

Cause me to walk in beauty, grace, mercy, holiness, humility, honor, love, peace, forgiveness, faith, truth, trust, willingness, compassion and obedience. (Galatians 5:16-25; 2 Timothy 2:20-24)

*Give me eyes ever to behold the red and purple sunset. (Jeremiah 9:25) Give me ears ever to hear the beautiful music sung by the birds, the wind and the rain. (Mark 9:20-27) Let me smell the aroma of the beautiful flowers. Let me experience the calmness in the ebb and flow of the waves at the shore and the peace in the roaring waters crashing against the rocks. (Matthew 8:26-27; John 14:27) Let me be lifted-up as the eagle by the aid of the mighty storm and hurricane that fiercely blow through the sky. (Isaiah 40:28-31) Make me wise so I may understand what You have taught me. (Proverbs 1:7) Help me learn the lessons You have hidden in every leaf and rock. (Proverbs 9:1-12)

Reveal to me the secrets hidden in Your word. (1 Corinthians 2:6-16) Remind me of truths that You have taught me, but I have neglected or forgotten. (John 14:25-26) *Show me Your ways, O Great Spirit. Teach me Your paths. Lead me in Your truth and teach me. For You are the God of my salvation. On You I wait all the day. (Psalm 25:4,5) Make me ready to come to You with clean hands, a pure heart and steady eyes, so that when life fades like the fading sunset, my spirit may come to You without shame. (2 Timothy 4:5-8) I gladly and willingly, submit, commit and dedicate my life to You. I surrender all to you. (Judges 17:3; John 15:19) Convince, convict, convert, redeem, recreate, consecrate and sanctify my heart and my life for humanity's great good and to Your greater glory. (1 Thessalonians 5:16-26) And this I ask in the name of Jesus Christ of Nazareth (Acts 3:6,16)

Amen

Adapted from the UMC HB #329 and #335
Pray this prayer every day
Annotated by Dr. Kwame O. Lartey
International House of Prayer Ministry
469-767-2926

PRAYER FOR GRACE TO BE CHRISTLIKE

*Father, the glorious God and Father of our Lord Jesus, grant me grace, through a living faith in Jesus Christ to be encouraged and filled with enthusiasm in all I do. May I be comforted knowing that Christ Jesus loves me dearly, and may I have a constant and consistent fellowship with the Holy Spirit, the Giver of life, our Advocate, Helper, Teacher, Comforter, and Strength. Grant me grace to be tenderhearted and compassionate in all my dealings with people. Through the power and efficacy of the Holy Spirit, grant me grace to believe and think, talk, and act like Jesus, to love like Jesus, and be one in spirit and purpose like Jesus, because I have the mind of Christ.
(1 Corinthians 2:16).*

*Grant that I may do nothing out of selfish ambition, or vain conceit, but that in humility I may consider others better than myself and put their needs and interests above mine. Grant me grace to have the same attitude that Christ Jesus had: "Who being the very nature and likeness of God, did not consider equality with God, something to be grasped, but made Himself nothing taking on the very nature of a servant, being made in human likeness, and being found in appearance as a man, He humbled Himself and became obedient unto death, even death on a cross. Therefore God exalted Him to the highest place and gave Him the name that is above every name, that at the name of Jesus every knee should bow in heaven and on earth, and under the earth, that every tongue should confess that Jesus Christ is Lord, to the glory of God the Father." Jesus, You are my Lord. You are my Savior, Priest and King. I believe in my heart that You are the Son of the Living God. The radiance of His glory, the exact image of His likeness.
(Hebrews 1:2,3).*

*I believe You were wounded for our transgressions. You were bruised for our iniquities, upon You was the chastisement that made us whole, and by Your stripes we were healed.
(Isaiah 53:4,5). I believe You were raised from the dead for our justification.
(Romans 4:20-25; 10:9,10).*

I also believe that You have redeemed us from the curse of the law by becoming a curse for us, for it is written, "Cursed be any one who hangs on a tree, so that we might receive the blessings of

Abraham and the gift of the Holy Spirit."
(Galatians 3:13,14).

Thank You, Lord Jesus for being my Savior, Redeemer, Healer and Deliverer.

*Jesus, You gave Your life for me; I give my life to You. (Isaiah 53; 1 Peter 2:19-25). I am no longer mine but Yours. Your life is my life, Your will is my will, Your way is my way, Your truth is my truth, Your people are my people. (John 14:1-14). Your plans and purposes are my plans and purposes. (Jeremiah 29:11; John 8:32-36). Anoint me with the Holy Spirit and with power so that I may go around doing good, and setting free all those oppressed by Satan because You are with me. Thank You Lord Jesus, I am now one with You and I have the person and power of the Holy Spirit. I am full of faith, power, love, wisdom, and of a sound mind.
(Matthew 3:11-12;
Acts 1:8, 6:5, 10:38;
1 Corinthians 12:13;
2 Timothy 1:6,7).

Thank You, Lord Jesus, for giving Your life for me.
(Matthew 8:16,17;
Galatians 3:13,14; 4:4-7).

Father, I willingly and gladly submit my life to You. I surrender my all to You. Convince, convict, convert, redeem, recreate, consecrate and sanctify my heart and my life for humanity's great good and to Your greater glory.
(Matthew 26:36-46;
1 Thessalonians 5:16-28).

*Daddy, enable me to be responsive to Your resurrection power so that each area of my life will be touched with hope and newness. Grant me grace to obey the leading and directions of the Holy Spirit, and to work out my own salvation with fear and trembling, knowing that it is God who works in me to will and act according to His good purpose. (John 11:25, 43, 44).

May I have the wisdom to do everything without complaining, arguing and grumbling.
(1 Corinthians 10:1-14), so that I may become blameless and pure, a child of God without fault in a crooked and depraved generation (world), so that I may shine like the stars in the universe, as I hold out the word of life, until the day I come to stand before Your throne of glory, to receive the crown of righteousness, together with all the saints.

This I ask in the name of Jesus, the Christ. (Philippians2:1-16, NIV, emphasis added)

Amen

Annotated by
Dr. Kwame O. Lartey
International House of Prayer
Ministry
469-767-2926

*Note: (*)

Pray these prayers every day. Pray the Prayer of the Holy Spirit before your studies, and then pray the prayer of Grace to be Christ Like after your studies. If these prayers are to long for you as a beginner, or if you don't have time to pray all these prayers at once, break them into little bitty pieces or segments.

For instance, start and end your prayers between each asterisk.

THE GOSPEL OF MATTHEW

Mary, the virgin and fiancée of Joseph finds out that she is going to have a baby by the Holy Spirit.

> "This was how the birth of Jesus Christ took place. His mother Mary was engaged to Joseph, but before they were married, she found out that she was going to have a baby by the Holy Spirit." Matthew 1:18

An Angel of the Lord reveals to Joseph, while he is contemplating divorce from Mary, that the child Mary is carrying was conceived by the Holy Spirit. He (the Angel) also reveals to Joseph what name is to be given the child after his birth.

> "Joseph was a man who always did what was right but he did not want to disgrace Mary publicly; so he made plans to break the engagement privately. While he was thinking about this, an angel of the Lord appeared to him in a dream and said "Joseph, descendant of David, do not be afraid to take Mary to be your wife. For it is by the Holy Spirit that she has conceived. She will have a son, and you will name Him Jesus—because He will save His people from their sins." Now all this happened in order to make come true what the Lord had said through the prophet. "A virgin will become pregnant and have a son, and He will be called Immanuel" (which means, God is with us) " Matthew 1:19-23

John, the prophet, and forerunner of Jesus tells the crowd he is baptizing in water but that one will come after him (Jesus), and baptize them in the Holy Spirit and fire. Because Jesus is to baptize believers in the Holy Spirit, He never baptized anyone in water. John 4:2

> "I baptize you with water to show that you have repented, but the one who will come after me will baptize you with the Holy Spirit and fire. He is much greater than I am; and

I am not good enough even to carry His sandals. He has His winnowing shovel with Him to thresh out all the grain. He will gather His wheat into His barn, but He will burn the chaff in a fire that never goes out." Matthew 3:11,12

Following Jesus' water baptism by John, the Holy Spirit descends like a dove on Him (visibly).

"As soon as Jesus was baptized, He came up out of the water. Then heaven was opened to Him and He saw the Spirit of God coming down like a dove and lighting on Him. Then a voice said from Heaven, "This is My own dear Son, with whom I am pleased" Matthew 3:16,17

The Spirit leads Jesus into the wilderness to be tempted by the Devil.

Then the Spirit led Jesus into the desert to be tempted by the Devil. "After spending forty days and nights without food, Jesus was hungry. Then the Devil came to Him and said: "If you are God's Son, order these stones to turn into bread" Matthew 4:1-3

Jesus tells the crowd that it is not by the power of Beelzebub (Satan) that He casts out demons, but by the power of the Holy Spirit.

"No, it is not Beelzebub, but God's Spirit, who gives Me the power to drive out demons, which proves that the Kingdom of God has already come upon you".
Matthew 12:28

Jesus tells the crowd of unbelievers and scoffers that every sin and blasphemy against the Holy Spirit will not be forgiven now or ever.

"For this reason I tell you: people can be forgiven any sin and any evil thing they say; but whoever says evil things against the Holy Spirit will not be forgiven. Anyone who says something against the Son of Man can be forgiven;

20

but whoever says something against the Holy Spirit will not be forgiven...now or ever." Matthew 12:31,32

The Spirit Inspires:

"Why then", Jesus asked, "did the Spirit inspire David to call Him Lord?" Matthew 22:43

Jesus was referring to David's prophecy about the Messiah. The prediction was the work of the Holy Spirit.

What Spirit did Jesus "yield" or breathe out during His death? Was it the Holy Spirit, or was it His human spirit? If you believe that Jesus was fully human, did He have a human spirit?

"Jesus again gave a loud cry and breathed His last." Matthew 27:50

Baptism in the name of the Holy Spirit

Jesus commanded His disciples "Go then to all peoples everywhere and make them my disciples. Baptize them in the name of the Father, the Son and the Holy Spirit." Matthew 28:19

The name of the Holy Spirit is to be included in the baptism of the believer. Does this strongly "suggest" that salvation is the work of the Father, Son and Holy Spirit?

Questions

1. How did Mary know that she was going to have a son by the Holy Spirit? Matthew 1:18-21; Luke 1:26-38
2. Has God ever revealed to you anything that He wanted you to know by dreams, visions, or revelation knowledge? Genesis 31:11-14; 37:5-11; 40:5-11;
Joel 2:28; Matthew 2:12
3. How do you prepare yourself to be a recipient of the above gifts? 1 Sam. 3:10; Psalm 119:18-20;
Ephesians 1:17-23; 2 Timothy 2:15-26; 3:16-17;
James 1:17-25; 1 Peter 1:21-22; 2 Peter 2:20-25
4. What is the difference between baptism with the Holy Spirit and fire, and water baptism? Matthew 3:11-17;
Mark 1:4-11; Luke 3:15-22; 4:16-28; Acts 1:5-8; 2:1-4
5. Have you been baptized by one or the other, or both? How do you receive either baptism? Matthew 7:7-11;
Luke 11:5-13; John 7:37-39
6. How do you overcome temptation, in your own strength or in the strength, power and wisdom of the Holy Spirit? Matthew 4:1-11; Luke 4:1-13; Galatians 5:15-26
7. When Jesus was tempted why did He quote scriptures? Was it not enough that He had fasted and been anointed by the Holy Spirit? Deuteronomy 8:3; Matthew 4:1-11; Ephesians 6:10-20; 2 Corinthians 10:3-6
8. What is blasphemy? Matthew 12:22-45. Can ordinary unbelievers be guilty of blasphemy? How about "true" believers? Hebrews 12:1-28
9. Why did King David call Jesus his Lord, even though Jesus was his "son"? Matthew 1:1; 20:29-32; Acts 2:32-36

THE GOSPEL OF MARK

Jesus will baptize believers with the Holy Spirit.

"I baptize you with water, but He will baptize you with the Holy Spirit" This is the testimony of John concerning Jesus. Jesus will baptize the believer with the Holy Spirit just as John is baptizing with water". Mark 1:8

Jesus is "baptized" with the Holy Spirit by God.

"As soon as Jesus came up out of the water, He saw the heaven opening and the Spirit coming down on Him like a dove. And a voice came from heaven, 'You are my own dear Son, I am pleased with you.'" Mark 1:10,11

The Spirit leads Jesus into the desert where He was tempted. Jesus was led into the wilderness by the Spirit so He could be fully prepared for His work.

"At once the Spirit made Him go into the desert where He stayed forty days being tempted by Satan." Mark 1:12

Sins against the Holy Spirit will not be forgiven.

"I assure you that people can be forgiven all their sins and all the evil things they may say. But whoever says evil things against the Holy Spirit will not be forgiven because he has committed an eternal sin." Mark 3:28,29

The Holy Spirit inspired David to say:

"The Lord said to my Lord, sit here at My right side until I put Your enemies under Your feet." Mark 12:36

The Holy Spirit will provide the right answer when the "Apostles" are arrested.

"And when you are arrested and taken to court, do not worry ahead of time about what you are going to say. When the time comes say whatever is then given to you.

For the words you speak will not be yours they will come from the Holy Spirit." Mark 13:11

Questions

1. As we noted in Matthew, there are two baptisms, water baptism and Holy Spirit baptism. Why are the mainline churches silent about the subject of baptism with the Holy Spirit (Mark 1:4-11) and are not teaching about the Holy Spirit? 1 Corinthians 14:1-5
2. Is the baptism in the Holy Spirit relevant to ministry and to the needs of the church today? Isaiah 61;
   Matthew 28:18-20; Luke 3:21,22; 4:14-19;
   Acts 2:1-47, 10:38; 1 Corinthians 12:8-14; 14:1-14
3. Who is responsible for water baptism in the church? Matthew 3:1-15; 28:19; Mark 1:1-11; 15:15,16;
   Luke 3:1-22; John 4:1-4
4. Who is responsible for Holy Spirit baptism in the church? Matthew 3:11-12; Mark 1:7-8;
   Acts 2:1-4; 8:14-24; 19:1-12; John 1:31-34; 4:1-3
5. Why was Jesus led by the Holy Spirit into the wilderness, where He fasted and afterwards He was tempted by Satan? Matthew 4:1-11; Mark 1:10-13; 4:1-11;
   Luke 4:4-13

The Gospel of Luke

The Holy Spirit will fill John with power from his birth.

"From his very birth he will be filled with the Holy Spirit and he will bring back many of the children of Israel to the Lord their God" Luke 1:15,16

The Holy Spirit will come upon Mary and make the conception of Jesus, the Word of God, the eternal, possible.

"The Holy Spirit will come on you, and God's power will rest upon you. For this reason the Holy Child will be called the "Son of God." Luke 1:35

The Holy Spirit filled Elizabeth and she spoke in a loud voice.

When Elizabeth heard Mary's greeting, the baby moved within her. Elizabeth was filled with the Holy Spirit and said in a loud voice, "You are the most blessed of all women and blessed is the child you will bear." Luke 1:41

Zachariah, the father of John, is filled with the Holy Spirit after his tongue is loosened and he prophesied.

"Let us praise the Lord the God of Israel. He has come to the help of His people and has set them free." Luke 1:67,68

The Holy Spirit was with Simeon, a God-fearing man, when He assured him that he would not die until he had seen Jesus, the Lord's promised Messiah. The Holy Spirit also led him into the temple when Jesus was brought there for the period of purification.

"The Holy Spirit was with him and assured him that he would not die before he had seen the Lord's promised Messiah. Led by the Spirit Simeon went into the temple." Luke 2:25-27

John was baptizing with water, but he told the people that the one who was coming after him, Jesus, will baptize with the Holy Spirit and with fire.

> "He will baptize you with the Holy Spirit and with fire."
> Luke 3:16

The Holy Spirit is descended on Jesus at His baptism

> "After all the people had been baptized, Jesus also was baptized. While He was praying, Heaven was opened, and the Holy Spirit came down upon Him in bodily form like a dove and a voice came from heaven saying, "You are my own dear Son, I am pleased with you."
> Luke 3:21,22

Filled with the Holy Spirit after His baptism, He was led by the Spirit into wilderness.

> "Jesus returned from the Jordan full of the Holy Spirit and was led by the Spirit into the desert where He was tempted by the Devil for forty days" Luke 4:1,2

After Jesus was tempted by the Devil, He returned to Galilee with the power of the Holy Spirit still with Him as He began His ministry.

> "And Jesus returned to Galilee and the power of the Holy Spirit was with Him." Luke 4:14

The scripture Jesus read before His ministry is indicative of the work of the Spirit. It sums up, In a nutshell, what the Spirit of the Lord is upon Jesus to enable Him to accomplish. This same Spirit will enable us, as God's ministers to accomplish these and more. (See John 14:12-14; 2 Corinthians 5:18-21)

> "The Spirit of the Lord is upon Me because He has chosen Me to bring good news to the poor. He has sent Me to bring liberty to the captives, and recovery of sight to the blind. To set free the oppressed and announce that the time has come when the Lord will save His people."
> Luke 4:18,19

The power of the Spirit was not only upon Him, i.e. in Him, but even His clothes were energized by His power. This scripture does not refer directly to the Holy Spirit, but it is implied. Jesus' healing ministry was accomplished by the power of the Holy Spirit. (See Luke 5:17-26; 8:40-56)

> "As the boy was coming the demon knocked him to the ground and threw him into a fit. Jesus gave a command to the evil spirit, healed the boy, and gave him to his father. <u>All the people were amazed at the mighty power of God</u>." That is the power of the Holy Spirit.
> Luke 9:42,43

The Holy Spirit fills Jesus with Joy

> At that time Jesus was filled with joy by the Holy Spirit and said "Father, Lord of heaven and earth, I thank You because You have shown to the unlearned what You have hidden from the wise and learned, Yes Father, this was how you were pleased to have it happen."
> Luke 10:21

The Father will give the Holy Spirit to those who ask Him, in Jesus name.

> "How much more then, will the Father in heaven give the Holy Spirit to those who ask Him?"
> Luke 11:13 (John 14:13,14; 16:23,24)

Jesus testifies that it is by the power of God (The Holy Spirit) that He drives out demons.

> "No rather it is by the means of God's power that I drive out demons and this proves that the Kingdom of God has already come to you."
> Luke 11:20 (John 14:13,14; 16:23,24)

Evil things said against the Holy Spirit will not be forgiven

> "Anyone who says a word against the Son of Man can be forgiven, but whoever says evil things against the Holy Spirit will not be forgiven." Luke 12:10

The Holy Spirit will teach the disciples what to say when they are brought to trial for preaching the word.

> "For the Holy Spirit will teach you at that time what to say." Luke 12:12

Jesus will send the promise of the Father from on high upon the disciples to be witnesses of these things.

> "And I myself will send upon you what my Father has promised. But you must wait in the city until the power from above comes down upon you." Luke 24:49

Questions

1. Why do we wait till birth and sometimes much later to ask God to fill our children with the Holy Spirit, when scripture tells us John the Baptist was filled with the Holy Spirit before his birth? Luke 1:15,16

2. The Holy Spirit is supposed to be our helper, comforter, counselor, teacher, etc. He is also supposed to inspire us to worship God in spirit and truth. Why is the majority of Christians ignorant of who the Holy Spirit is and the role He plays in our lives? (Many refer to Him as "it" or a "she" i.e. a goddess, or a power, not a person with power.) John 4:22-24; 14

3. Do you believe in the Holy Spirit and are you one with Him? Does He inspire you to worship, praise and exalt God in spirit and in truth? John 4:23,24, 14:15-17; 1 Corinthians 12:13

4. According to Luke, what did God anoint Jesus to do? What Old Testament scripture was Jesus quoting? Isaiah 61:1-4; Luke 4:14-19

5. Can you be anointed (baptized with the Holy Spirit and fire) to do what Jesus was anointed to do? Luke 11:5-13; John 14:12-14; 16:23-24; Ephesians 1:15-23; 3:14-21

6. What is the sure way to know who Jesus is? Matthew 16: 15-19; Luke 2:25-31; Acts 9:3-20

THE GOSPEL OF JOHN

John's testimony about how he came to know that Jesus Christ is the Son of God. The Spirit revealed Jesus to him and God, through the Spirit, spoke to him and confirmed it.

"And John gave the testimony, "I saw the Spirit come down like a dove from Heaven and stayed on Him. I still did not know that He was the one, but God, who sent me to baptize with water, had said to me "You will see the Spirit come down and stay on a man: He is the one who baptizes with the Holy Spirit." I have seen it, said John, and I tell you that He is the Son of God." John 1:32-34

A person must be born into God's kingdom, God's family, by water and the Spirit."

"I am telling you the truth" replied Jesus, "that no one can enter the kingdom of God unless he is born of water and the Spirit." A person is born physically of human parents, but he is born spiritually of the Spirit. Do not be surprised that I tell you that you must be born again. The wind blows where it wishes, you hear the sound it makes, but you do not know where it comes from or where it is going. It is like that with everyone who is born of the Spirit" John 3:5-8

John the Baptist gives more testimony about Jesus and confirms that He is the Son of God, because God has given Him the fullness of His Spirit.

"He tells what He has seen and heard, yet no one accepts His message. But whoever accepts His message confirms by this that God is truthful. The one whom God has sent speaks God's word because God gave him the fullness of His Spirit." John 3:32-34

The Spirit will enable people to worship God as He really is.

"But the time is coming and is already here when, by the power of God's Spirit, people will worship the Father as He really is, offering Him the true worship that He wants." John 4:23

God is Spirit

"God is Spirit and only by the power of His Spirit can people worship Him as He really is." John 4:24

The Spirit gives life to all believers

"What gives life is God's Spirit; man's power is of no use at all. The words I have spoken to you brings God's life-giving Spirit. Yet some of you do not believe." John 6:63

The Spirit is like water that quenches the thirst of those who are thirsty. There is a spiritual thirst in all human beings, and the Spirit will quench that thirst.

On the last and most important day of the festival, Jesus stood up and said in a loud voice "Whoever is thirsty must come to Me and drink. As the scripture says, whoever believes in Me streams of life-giving water will pour out from his heart. Jesus said this about the Spirit, which those who believe in Him were going to receive. At that time the Spirit had not yet been given, because Jesus had not been raised to glory." John 7:37-39

The Spirit is our helper and comforter. He is also the revealer of God's truth and He will stay with the believer forever.

"If you love Me you will obey my commandments. I will ask the Father and He will give you another helper who will stay with you forever. He is the Spirit who reveals the truth about God. The world cannot receive Him because it cannot see Him or know Him. But you know Him because He remains with you and is in you." John 14:15-17

The Holy Spirit is not only our helper, helping us to overcome all the trials, tribulations and troubles of this world; He is also our teacher for excellence and will help us remember the teachings and sayings of Jesus.

> I have told you this while I am still with you. The Helper, the Holy Spirit, whom the Father will send in my name will teach you everything, and make you remember all that I have told you." John 14:25,26

The Spirit comes from the Father and is sent to us by <u>Jesus</u> and His purpose is to reveal Jesus and speak to us about Jesus.

> "The Helper will come, the Spirit who reveals the truth about God; and who comes from the Father. I will send Him to you from the Father, and He will speak about Me. And you too will speak about Me, because you have been with Me from the very beginning." John 15:26

The Spirit will come after Jesus goes away

> "But I am telling you the truth. It is better for you that I go away, because if I do not go the Helper will not come to you. For if I do go away, then I will send Him to you" John 16:7

This verse also indicates that Jesus will send the Spirit. The Spirit will prove to the world about sin and vindicate Jesus as the righteous one.

> "And when He comes He will prove to the people of the world that they are wrong about sin, because they do not believe in Me, they are wrong about what is right because I am going to the Father and you will not see Me
> anymore and they are wrong about judgment, because the ruler of this world has already been judged."
> John 16:8-11

The Spirit will reveal to the disciples the truth about God and give them the mental capacity and capability to remember.

"I have much to tell you but now it would be too much for you to bear. When, however, the Spirit comes—who reveals the truth about God, He will lead you into all the truth." John 16:12,13

The Spirit will not speak on His own authority, and He will also speak of things to come.

"He will not speak on His own authority, but will speak of what He hears and will tell you of things to come." John 16:13

The Spirit will glorify Jesus by saying what Jesus says.

"He will give Me glory because He will take what I say and tell it to you. All that my Father has is mine that is why I said that the Spirit will take what I give Him and tell it to you." John 16:14,15

Jesus is the giver of the Holy Spirit. Through the Holy Spirit, the disciples will be able to forgive or not to forgive sins.

"Then He breathed on them and said, 'Receive the Holy Spirit. If you forgive people's sins they are forgiven. If you do not forgive them, they are not forgiven.'" John 20:22,23

Questions

1. How is Jesus revealed to us? John 1:31-36
2. How is a person born into the Kingdom of God?
   John 3:3-13
3. How is such a person described in scripture, or what is he/she called? Romans 8:8-16; 10:9,10;
   2 Corinthians 5:17-21
4. How does God give His Spirit to us? John 3:31-36
5. When did God make His Spirit available to all believers? John 7:37-39
6. Who is qualified to receive the Holy Spirit and His baptism? John 14:15-17
7. Who is the Holy Spirit? John 14:16-17, 26; 15:26; 16:7; Romans 8
8. What role does the Holy Spirit play in our lives when He comes to dwell in us? John 14:15-17, 26; 16:7-15
9. Make a careful note of the language (pronouns and adjectives) Jesus uses to talk about the Holy Spirit. Is the Holy Spirit and Jesus the same person? Dig a little deeper and examine again the question: Who is the Holy Spirit? John 16:7; Romans 8:1-27
10. Who is responsible for sending the Holy Spirit to us? John 16:7
11. What does the Spirit convict the world of? What does He reprove the world of? John 16:8-12
12. How does John's gospel help us to understand the doctrine of the Trinity or God in three persons, but one (Trinity)? John 14:1-14 (also refer carefully to the other scriptures quoted above)
13. After His resurrection, what did Jesus do to impart the Holy Spirit to us believers? John 20:22

14. From the above scriptures, what is your role and responsibility for the presence of the Holy Spirit in your life?

The Book of The Acts of the Apostles

Instruction is given by Jesus to His disciples (apostles) by the power of the Holy Spirit.

> "Before He was taken up He gave instructions by the power of the Holy Spirit to the men He had chosen as His apostles." Acts 1:2

Baptism with the Holy Spirit is a gift from the Father promised by Him.

> "Do not leave Jerusalem but wait for the gift. I told you about, the gift my Father promised. John baptized with water but; in a few days you will be baptized with the Holy Spirit." Acts 1:4,5

It is significant to note that the baptism with the Holy Spirit will not be given until they waited as the Lord commanded them.

The power of the Holy Spirit is received by baptism. The apostles will be baptized with the Holy Spirit. He is like a river into which the apostles will be immersed.
The purpose of the baptism of the Holy Spirit is to fill the apostles with power (Dunamis) to be able to bear witness of Jesus, by word and deed (preaching, healing, teaching, casting out of demons, and acting in love) in all the regions surrounding them and beyond.

> "But when the Holy Spirit comes upon you, you will be filled with power, and you will be witnesses for Me in Jerusalem, in all Judea, and Samaria and to the ends of the earth." Acts 1:8

The Holy Spirit spoke through David (the prophet, priest and King)

> "My brothers", he said, "The scripture had to come true in which the Holy Spirit speaking through David made a

prediction about Judas who was the guide for those who arrested Jesus." Acts 1:16

The Holy Spirit employs the properties of the wind (a mighty wind) and fire for His work because He is the wind and the fire of God. The Holy Spirit gives utterance to the disciples baptized in His power to speak in other languages. Note that the disciples did the talking and not the Holy Spirit, i.e., the Holy Spirit employed their tongues. The disciples did the speaking (Evidence to their minds that they have power and that a miracle has taken place).

> "When the day of Pentecost came, all the believers were gathered together in one place. Suddenly, there was a noise from the sky which sounded like a strong wind blowing, and it filled the whole house where they were sitting. Then they saw what looked like tongues' of fire which spread out and touched each person there. They were all filled with the Holy Spirit and began to talk in other languages, as the Spirit enabled them to speak." Acts 2:1-4

The baptism of the Spirit enables one to prophesy; see visions; and dream dreams. The Spirit is the originator of the miracles in the sky, and on earth and all the strange occurrences before the coming judgment of God.

> "Instead, this is what the prophet Joel spoke about." (through the power of the Holy Spirit). "This is what I will do in the last days; God says I will pour out my Spirit on everyone. Your sons and your daughters will proclaim my message; your young men will see visions and your old men will have dreams. Yes even on my servants, both men and women I will pour out my Spirit in those days, and they will proclaim my message." Acts 2:16-18

Jesus received the Holy Spirit from the Father after His resurrection, according to God's promise, and Jesus, in turn, gives us the Spirit.

"He has been raised to the right hand of God, His Father, and has received from Him the Holy Spirit as He had promised. What you now see and hear is His gift that He has poured out on us." Acts 2:33

The gift of the Spirit, that is the baptism with the Holy Spirit, can be received immediately after water baptism, after one has received forgiveness for his or her sins.

"Each one of you must turn away from your sins and be baptized in the name of Jesus Christ, so that your sins will be forgiven and you will receive God's gift, the Holy Spirit. For God's promise was made to you and your children and to all who are far away—all whom the Lord our God calls to Himself." Acts 2:38,39

The Holy Spirit gives courage and boldness to Peter to answer the High Priest and his court. Acts 4:13

"Peter, full of the Holy Spirit, answered them "Leaders of the People and elders; if we are being questioned today about the good deed done to the lame man and how he was healed, then you should all know, and all the people of Israel should know that this man stands here before you completely well through the power of the name of Jesus Christ of Nazareth—whom you crucified and whom God raised from death." Acts 4:8-10

The Holy Spirit spoke through the prophets and all the holy men of God.

"Master and Creator of heaven, earth and sea and all that is in them! By means of the Holy Spirit you spoke through our ancestor David, your servant."
Acts 4:24b-25a

The Holy Spirit can demonstrate His invisible presence through earthquakes, and the unusual boldness He gives to those baptized or anointed.

> "When they finished praying the place where they were meeting was shaken. They were filled with the Holy Spirit and began to proclaim God's message with boldness." Acts 4:31

The Holy Spirit gives knowledge of the deceitfulness of Ananias and Saphira, his wife, to Peter. They lied to the Holy Spirit.

> Peter said to him, "Ananias, why did you let Satan take control of you and make you lie to the Holy Spirit by keeping part of the money you received for the property." Acts 5:3

Peter, in speaking to Saphira, demonstrates that their deceitfulness was a test of the Holy Spirit.

> So Peter said to her, "Why did you and your husband decide to put the Lord's Spirit to the test." Acts 5:9

Peter, in speaking to the High Priest and his party, says the Holy Spirit is a witness of the deeds and resurrection of Jesus, and that He is a gift from God to those who obey Him. The Holy Spirit is not for certain groups of people in a denomination; He is for all God's obedient children.

> "We are witnesses to these things-we and the Holy Spirit, who is God's gift to those who obey Him." Acts 5:32

The Apostles choose men who are full of the Holy Spirit and wisdom to be deacons.

> "So then, brothers and sisters choose seven men among you who are known to be full of the Holy Spirit and wisdom, and we will put them in charge of this matter." Acts 6:3

Stephen, a man of faith and of the Holy Spirit is chosen as one of the seven deacons

"The whole group was pleased with the apostles' proposal, so they chose Stephen, a man full of faith and the Holy Spirit." Acts 6:5

The Spirit gives wisdom to Stephen to withstand his enemies.

"But the Spirit gave Stephen such wisdom that when he spoke they could not refute him." (See the evidence of this in verse 15) Acts 6:10

Stephen, in his defense, accused the Israelites of resisting the Holy Spirit.

"You are just like your ancestors: you too have always resisted the Holy Spirit. Was there any prophet that your ancestors did not persecute? They killed God's messengers, who long ago announced the coming of His righteous servant." Acts 7:51d-52c

The Holy Spirit enabled Stephen to see the Glory of God.

"But Stephen full of the Holy Spirit, looked up to heaven and saw God's Glory and Jesus standing at the right side of God: 'Look', he said, 'I see heaven opened and the Son of Man standing at the right side of God'."
Acts 7:55-56

Peter and John prayed for the believers in Samaria to receive baptism with the Holy Spirit. After they had prayed, they laid their hands on them to receive and they did.

"When they arrived they prayed for the believers that they might receive the Holy Spirit. For the Holy Spirit had not yet come down on any of them, they had only been baptized in the name of the Lord Jesus. Then Peter and John placed their hands on them and they received the Holy Spirit" Acts 8:15-17

Peter rebukes Simon the magician for wanting to receive the gift of the Holy Spirit with money.

> "Simon saw that the Spirit had been given to the believers when the apostles placed their hands on them. So he offered money to Peter and John and said, 'Give this power to me too, so that anyone I place my hands on will receive the Holy Spirit.' But Peter answered him, 'May you and your money go to hell for thinking that you can buy God's gift with money. You have no part or share in our work, because your heart is not right in God's sight.'" Acts 8:18-21

Note that Peter indicates in verses 21-22 that the Holy Spirit can be received only by those whose hearts are right before God; those who truly repent of their sins. This means the in-filling of the Holy Spirit after water baptism (Galatians 5:16-22) and the visible anointing of the Holy Spirit, which occurred almost immediately after water baptism, in the early church.

The Holy Spirit prompts Philip—speaks to him—to go and talk to the Ethiopian eunuch.

> "The Holy Spirit said to Philip, "Go over to that carriage and stay close to it." Acts 8:29

The Holy Spirit transports Philip from Gaza to Ashdod.

> "When they came up out of the water, the Spirit of the Lord took Philip away. The official did not see him again, but continued on his way full of joy. Philip found himself in Ashdod." Acts 8:39,40

The Lord Jesus sends Ananias to pray for Saul so that he may see again and receive the Holy Spirit by the laying on of hands.

> "So Ananias went and entered the house where Saul was and placed his hands on him 'Brother Saul', he said, 'The Lord has sent me, Jesus Himself, who appeared to you on the road, as you were coming here. He sent me so that

you might see again and be filled with the Holy Spirit.'"
Acts 9:17

Note: Saul received the baptism of the Holy Spirit before he was baptized in water. Verse 18

The church in Judea, Galilee, and Samaria was strengthened by the Holy Spirit and it grew in numbers.
> "And so it was that the Church throughout Judea, Galilee and Samaria had a time of peace. Through the help of the Holy Spirit, it was strengthened and grew in numbers as it lived in reverence for the Lord" Acts 9:31

The Spirit speaks to Peter and tells him to go with the men sent by Cornelius because He sent them.
> "Peter was still trying to understand what the vision meant. When the Spirit said, "Listen, three men are here looking for you, so get ready and go down and do not hesitate to go with them for I have sent them."
> Acts 10:19-20

Peter indicates in his speech at Cornelius's house that it was God who poured the Holy Spirit on Jesus, for doing good and for healing all who are under the power of Satan
> "You know about Jesus of Nazareth, and how God poured out on Him the Holy Spirit and power. He went everywhere doing good, and healing all who are under the power of the Devil for God was with Him" Acts 10:38

The Holy Spirit is poured upon the household of Cornelius even before they are baptized in water, while Peter is telling them the good news.
> "While Peter was still speaking, the Holy Spirit came down on all those who were listening to his message." Acts 10:44

Note that here; speaking in tongues follows the baptism of the Holy Spirit.

"The Jewish believers who had come from Joppa with Peter were amazed that God had poured out His gift of the Holy Spirit on the Gentiles also. For they heard them speaking in strange tongues and praising God's greatness. Peter spoke up, 'These people have received the Holy Spirit just as we did. Can anyone then stop them from being baptized with water?' So he ordered them to be baptized in the name of Jesus Christ."
Acts 10:45-48

Peter recounts how the Spirit asked him to go with the messengers from Cornelius without hesitation.

"The Spirit told me to go without hesitation." Acts 11:12

He recounts again how the Holy Spirit came upon Cornelius' household.

"And when I began to speak, the Holy Spirit came down on them, just as on us at the beginning. Then I remembered what the Lord had said. 'John baptized with water, but you will be baptized with the Holy Spirit.'" Acts 11:15,16

With the power of the Holy Spirit, many people were brought to the Lord.

"Barnabas was a good man, full of the Holy Spirit and faith and many people were brought to the Lord. "
Acts 11:24

Through the power of the Holy Spirit, Agabus makes a prediction.

"One of them named Agabus, stood up and by the power of the Spirit predicted that a severe famine was about to come over all the earth." Acts 11:28

The Holy Spirit speaks to the prophets and teachers in Antioch to set apart Barnabas and Saul while they are fasting.

"While they were serving the Lord and fasting, the Holy Spirit said to them, 'Set apart for me Barnabas and Saul to do the work to which I have called them.'" Acts 13:2

The Holy Spirit chooses the itinerary of Saul and Barnabas

"Having been sent by the Holy Spirit, Barnabas and Saul went to Seleucia and sailed from there to the Island of Cyprus." Acts 13:4

By the power of the Holy Spirit, Saul, for the first time called Paul, discerns the evil machinations of the magician at Paphos, by name Elymas (Sergius Paulus).

"Then Saul-also known as Paul- was filled with the Holy Spirit, he looked straight at the magician, and said "you son of the Devil! You are the enemy of everything that is good. You are full of all kinds of evil tricks and you always keep trying to turn the Lord's truth into lies. The Lord's hand will come down on you now, you will be blind and will not see the light of day for a time."
Acts 13:9-11

The Holy Spirit fills the believers with joy.

"The believers in Antioch were full of joy and the Holy Spirit" Acts 13:52

Peter testifies in the Council of Jerusalem that God showed His approval of the Gentiles by giving His Spirit to them, when they believed, repented and were baptized.

"And God who knows the thought of everyone, showed His approval of the Gentiles by giving the Holy Spirit to them, just as He did to us. He made no difference between them and us. He forgave their sins because they believed." Acts 15:8,9

The Council in Jerusalem concluded their deliberation and wrote a letter convinced that it was the will of the Holy Spirit, coupled with their own experience, that the Jewish Christians do not demand that the Gentile Christians obey the Mosaic Law.

"The Holy Spirit and we have agreed not to put any other burden on you besides these necessary rules: eat no food that has been offered to idols; eat no blood; eat no animals that have been strangled; and keep yourselves from sexual immorality." Acts 15:28,29

The Holy Spirit specifically chooses the preaching itinerary of Paul, making sure that he preaches in the areas He wants him to. (There are specific things the Holy Spirit would like us to do at some specific times and places. Certain peoples He likes us to see, and even what He wants us to say to them and how it is all a matter of being obedient to the Holy Spirit).

"They traveled through the region of Phrygia and Galatia because the Holy Spirit did not let them preach the message in the province of Asia. When they reached the border of Mysia, they tried to go into the province of Bithynia, but the Spirit of Jesus did not allow them." Acts 16:6,7 (read also 16:8-10; 18:9,10)

Paul meets some believers in Ephesus and baptizes them in the Holy Spirit, who after receiving the baptism in the Holy Spirit spoke in tongues

"While Apollos was in Corinth, Paul traveled through the interior of the province and arrived in Ephesus. There he found some disciples and asked them, 'Did you receive the Holy Spirit when you became believers?' 'We have not even heard that there is a Holy Spirit,' they answered. 'Well, then, what kind of baptism did you receive?' Paul asked. 'The baptism of John', they answered. Paul said, 'The baptism of John was for those who turned from their sins; and he told the people of Israel to believe in the one who was coming after him -that is, in Jesus'. When they heard this, they were baptized in the name of the Lord Jesus. Paul placed his hands on them, and the Holy Spirit came upon them, they spoke in strange tongues, and also proclaimed God's message. There were about twelve men in all." Acts 19:1-7

Paul hears and obeys the Holy Spirit in his ministry.

"And now, in obedience to the Holy Spirit, I am going to Jerusalem not knowing what will happen to me there. I only know that in every city the Holy Spirit has warned me that prison and troubles wait for me. But I reckon my own life to be worth nothing to me, I only want to complete my mission and finish the work that the Lord Jesus gave me to do, which is to declare the good news about the grace of God." Acts 20:22-24

Paul teaches that the Holy Spirit places in the care of the leaders of the church, the "flock".

"So keep watch over yourselves and over all the flock which the Holy Spirit has placed in your care. Be shepherds of the church of God, which He made His –own through the death of His Son." Acts 20:28

The believers in Tyre knew by the Spirit what was going to happen to Paul in Jerusalem and they tried to persuade him not to go.

"By the power of the Spirit they told Paul not to go to Jerusalem, but when our time with them was over, we left and went on our way." All their wives and children went with us out of the city to the beach where we knelt and prayed." Acts 21:4b-5

In Caesarea a prophet by the name of Agabus demonstrated what was going to happen to Paul in Jerusalem, by the power of the Holy Spirit.

"We had been there for several days when a prophet named Agabus arrived from Judea. He came to us, took Paul's belt, tied up his own hands and feet with it and said, 'This is what the Holy Spirit says: the owner of this belt will be tied up In this way by the Jews in Jerusalem and they will hand him over to the Gentiles.'"
Acts 21:10,11 (read also Acts 23:11)

Paul concludes after talking to the Jews in Rome that what the Holy Spirit said about them through the Prophet Isaiah was true.

"So they left disagreeing among themselves, after Paul had said this one thing,: "How well the Holy Spirit spoke through Isaiah to your ancestors, for He said, "Go and say to this people, you will listen and listen, but not understand, you will look and look but not see, because the people's minds are dull, and they have stopped up their ears and closed their eyes" Otherwise their eyes would see, their ears would hear, their minds would understand, and they would turn to Me, says God, and I would heal them." Acts 28:25-27

Questions

Note: Many believers depict the Book of Acts, as "The Acts of the Holy Spirit". In many ways, they are right. The Book of Acts has more references about the Holy Spirit than any other book in the Bible.

1. Why is the person and power of the Holy Spirit a gift to the body of Christ? Acts 1:2
   (Note: As you study Acts, pay attention to how the Holy Spirit is depicted, not just as a "power", but as a person who speaks, directs, guides, hears, listens, sees, knows, and can predict accurately events about to happen). Acts 1:8; 5:9; 8:15-17

2. What is the purpose of the empowerment promised in Acts 1:8?

3. Do we need empowerment or the "baptism" or the anointing of the Holy Spirit in the church today? Matthew 28:18-20; Mark 16:14-20;
   1 Corinthians 14:1-4

4. What is the purpose of tongues? Are tongues for today's church or were they only for the early church? Acts 2:1-4 (read the entire chapter 2);
   1 Corinthians 12:8-12; 14:1-14

5. Do we need the baptism or empowerment of the Holy Spirit for our personal salvation or redemption? (Read the entire chapters of Galatians 4 and
   1 Corinthians 12-14. The Corinthian church was having some of the same problems we have about baptism in the Holy Spirit and tongues. These chapters, prayerfully read with the help of the Holy Spirit and an unbiased book or teaching on the Holy Spirit, will correctly help answer the above questions).

6. After reading and studying these scriptures, what is your decision? Do you want the baptism with the Holy Spirit, yes or no?

7. How do you receive this gift if you want it?

Acts 2:1-4; 8:14-17; 19:1-7 (If you sincerely want this gift, ask Jesus to baptize you – He is the baptizer, Mark 1:7, 8, and then turn your tongue loose to the Holy Spirit, He will give you the utterance. Acts 2:1-4)

Note carefully also that the early church did not start evangelizing their world until this empowerment. Paul did not start his ministry without the Holy Spirit. Acts 1:8; 9:17,18

8. What role does the Holy Spirit and His empowering play in church growth?
Acts 2:41,47; 6:1; 9:31; 10:19-20

9. In the first general conference of the early church, whose leadership and guidance did the church follow? Acts 15:28,29; 20:22-24

10. Why did Paul baptize believers who had received the teaching and baptism of John again in water and then with the Holy Spirit? Acts 9:1-7

11. Did you receive the baptism of the Holy Spirit with the evidence of speaking in tongues, when you believed? Acts 10:44-47, 11:12-18

THE BOOK OF ROMANS

The Work of the Spirit in the Christian

Paul reveals that true circumcision, i.e. Spiritual circumcision, is the work of the Holy Spirit—God's Spirit.

> "After all is a real Jew truly circumcised? It is not the man who is a Jew on the outside whose circumcision is a physical thing. Rather, the real Jew is the person who is a Jew on the inside, that is, whose heart has been circumcised, and this is the work of God's Spirit, not of the written Law. Such a person receives his praise from God, not from man." Romans 2:28,29 (refer also to Romans 1:16, 17, there is power, Holy Spirit power, in the gospel to save us.)

Paul speaks about our boasting in hope of sharing in God's Glory in Romans 5:2, which hope is given to us by God pouring out His love in our hearts, through His Spirit, who is God's gift to us who believe.

> "This Hope does not disappoint us, for God has poured out His love within our hearts by means of the Holy Spirit who is God's gift to us" Romans 5:5

The work of the Spirit in the believer

Paul theologizes that it is the law of the Spirit of life, which sets us free from the law of sin and death.

> "There is no condemnation now for those who live in union with Christ Jesus. For the law of the Spirit which brings us life in union with Christ Jesus has set me free from the law of sin and death." Romans 8:1,2

Paul, again, teaches that sin has been crucified through the life, death, and resurrection of Jesus Christ, God's Son, who took upon Him our nature in order to do away with sin. God did this

so that we might die to sin and be recreated in the nature of God, by His Spirit, who gives us life, to satisfy the righteous demands of the law.

> "What the Law could not do because human nature was weak, God did. He condemned sin in human nature, by sending His own Son, who came with a nature like man's sinful nature, to do away with sin. God did this so the righteous demands of the Law might be fully satisfied in us who live according to the Spirit, and not according to the human nature. Those who live as their human nature tells them to, have their minds controlled by what human nature wants. Those who live as the Spirit tells them to - have their minds controlled by what the Spirit wants."
> Romans 8:3-5

Note: The end result of what Paul is saying is that the Spirit gives life, but that sin (Law of sin) breeds death—see also Romans 6:23.

> "To be controlled by human nature results in death, to be controlled by the Spirit results in life and peace."
> Romans 8:6

Again, Paul propounds that if the Spirit lives in us, through faith in Jesus, we will love according to the demands of the Spirit— we will be submitted to the righteous demands of the Spirit, and not the wicked demands of sin. The line is therefore drawn. It is the Spirit of Christ, who enables us to live a righteous life; therefore if we do not have Christ's Spirit, we do not belong to Him.

> "But you do not live as your human nature tells you to, instead you live as the Spirit tells you to - if in fact God's Spirit lives in you. Whoever does not have the Spirit of Christ does not belong to Him." Romans 8:9

Continuing in verse 10-11, Paul teaches that accepting Christ as our Savior brings the Spirit into our lives, who gives to us life—

Note: where Christ is the Spirit is also and vice versa. The Spirit and Christ are not the same, but they are one. They are inseparable, just as my heart is inseparable from my lungs. I cannot live without a lung or heart; I need both to survive. The Spirit also in us, is an indication that we have been put right with God—reconciled to God. This does not mean that our physical bodies will not die, we will still die because of sin, but we will be raised to life-eternal, just as Jesus was raised to life through the power of the Spirit. Our physical bodies will be raised to life not our spiritual bodies, because our spirits have been crucified and made anew. Galatians 2:19, 20; 2 Corinthians 5:17

> "But if Christ lives in you, the Spirit is life for you, because you have been put right with God, even though your bodies are going to die because of sin. If the Spirit of God, who raised Jesus from death lives in you, then He who raised Christ from death, will also give life to your mortal bodies by the presence of His Spirit in you."
> Romans 8:10,11

By the power of God's Spirit, we put to death our sinful human nature and pass on to life, life eternal.

> "For if you live according to your human nature, you are going to die, but if by the Spirit you put to death your sinful actions, you will live." Romans 8:13

Again, Paul explains that the Spirit in-dwelling in us believers creates us into God's children, God's sons and daughters. The Spirit in us actually makes us cry out from deep within our souls and our spirits, (Luke 15:11-32) "Father, my Father", and this same Spirit bears witness—give us a deep inner conviction that we are God's children. The Spirit as God's gift to us is God's iron clad guarantee that we shall share in His glory.

> "Those who are led by God's Spirit are God's sons. For the Spirit, that God has given you, does not make you slaves and cause you to be afraid; instead the Spirit makes you God's children. By the Spirit's power we cry out to God,

'Father! My Father'. God's Spirit joins Himself to our spirit to declare that we are God's children. Since we are His children we will possess the blessings He keeps for His people, and we will also possess with Christ what God has kept for Him; for if we share Christ's suffering we shall also share His glory." Romans 8:14-17

Paul explains further that the hope, which God implants in our hearts by the power of the Spirit, makes us yearn for a final and total liberation, together with all creation.
But it is not just creation alone which groans, we who have the Spirit as the first fruits of God's gifts also groan within ourselves as we wait for God to make us His sons and daughters and sets our whole being free.
Meanwhile, the Spirit Intercedes for us, helps us in our weaknesses, pleads for us before God, and even forms the words that are in our innermost being, i.e. in our spirit or heart- - that we cannot sense, see, or express, using the prayer language of the Spirit—and ordinarily prays for us, to plead with God in accordance with His will.

"In the same way the Spirit also comes to help us, weak as we are. For we do not know how we ought to pray; the Spirit Himself pleads with God for us in groans that words cannot express. And God, who sees into our hearts, knows what the thought of the Spirit is, because the Spirit pleads with God on behalf of His people and in accordance with His will." Romans 8:23,26

Paul declares that the Holy Spirit rules his conscience.

"I am speaking the truth: I belong to Christ and I do not lie. My conscience, ruled by the Holy Spirit, also assures me that I am not lying when I say how great is my sorrow, how endless the pain in my heart for my people, my own flesh and blood! For their sakes, I could wish that I myself were under God's curse and separated from Christ." Romans 9:1-3

Paul teaches that "righteousness, peace and joy" are gifts of the Holy Spirit.

"For God's kingdom is not a matter of eating and drinking, but of righteousness, peace and joy which the Holy Spirit gives. And when someone serves Christ in this way, he pleases God and is approved by others."
Romans 14:17,18

Paul prays that the Roman church may grow in hope by the power of the Holy Spirit.

"May God the source of hope, fill you with all joy and peace by means of your faith in Him, so that your hope will continue to grow by the power of the Holy Spirit."
Romans 15:13

Paul serves as priest in preaching so that the Gentiles may be acceptable to God, dedicated to Him by the Holy Spirit.

"I serve like a priest in preaching the Good News from God, in order that the Gentiles may be an offering acceptable to God dedicated to Him by the Holy Spirit."
Romans 15:16

Paul declares that Christ, through the power of the Holy Spirit, enables him, Paul, to lead the Gentiles to obey God, to speak boldly, and to perform deeds of courage, miracles, and wonders.

"I will be bold and speak only about what Christ has done through me to lead the Gentiles to obey God. He has done this by means of words and deeds, by the power of miracles and wonders, and by the power of the Spirit of God." Romans 15:18,19

Paul propounds that love is a gift of the Holy Spirit.

"I urge you, brothers by our Lord Jesus Christ, and by the love that the Spirit gives join me in praying fervently to God for me." Romans 15:30

Questions

1. What makes the difference between an unbelieving Christian and a believing Christian? The one who is under the Law of sin and death and the one under the Law of the Spirit of life? Romans 2:28,29; 8:1,2
2. How is the difference clearly demonstrated? Romans 8:3-17
3. What is Christian hope and why can we not be disappointed by believing and expecting this hope to be fulfilled in its appointed time? Romans 5:1-11
4. What is our Christian responsibility, obligation, and discipline to allow the Holy Spirit to continue to guide us, teach us, counsel us, empower us, strengthen us, and comfort us daily? Romans 9:1-3,8,32-33; 10:5-13,17
5. What is true peace? Do you have peace and joy in your spirit? Peace in your mind? How do you get this peace? Romans 14:16-23; Philippians 4:4-9
6. In light of all the turmoil, violence, terrorism, destruction, and death all over the world, do you have genuine hope, steadfast confidence, and confident expectation that God is in control and will take care of you no matter where you go and no matter what happens? Who empowers you and strengthens you to have this hope, this confidence? Romans 15:13,16,18-19,30-33 (continually ask for this hope to be strengthened. Matthew 7:7-8)

THE BOOK OF I CORINTHIANS

True preaching, Paul shows, must be accompanied by the convincing proof of the power of God's Spirit.
> "So when I came to you, I was weak and trembled all over with fear and my teaching and message were not delivered with skillful words of human wisdom, but with convincing proof of the power of God's Spirit. Your faith then does not rest on human wisdom but on God's power."
> 1 Corinthians 2:3-5 (see also 1 Corinthians 1:18-25)

God's self-revelation is made to us through His Spirit, as Paul correctly teaches. For the Spirit of God knows all about God, and is therefore able to reveal everything to us.
> "But it was to us that God made known His secret, by means of His Holy Spirit. The Spirit searches everything even the hidden depths of God's purposes. It is only a person's own spirit within him that knows all about him, In the same way, only God's Spirit knows all about God. We have not received this world's spirit; instead, we have received the Spirit sent by God, so that we may know all that God has given us."   1 Corinthians 2:10-12

If we are led and inspired by the Spirit then what we say and teach come from the Spirit of God and it is only those who have the Spirit that can understand and receive these teachings. And whoever has the Spirit has received the mind of Christ.
> "So then we do not speak in words taught by human wisdom, but in words taught by the Spirit, as we explain spiritual truths to those who have the Spirit. Whoever does not have the Spirit cannot receive the gifts that come from God's Spirit. Such a person does not really understand them; they are nonsense to him, because their value can be judged only on a spiritual basis.

Whoever has the Spirit however is able to judge the value of everything, but no one is able to judge him, as the scripture says: 'Who knows the mind of the Lord? Who is able to give Him advice? We, however, have the mind of Christ.'" 1 Corinthians 2:13-16

We cannot teach people who do not have the Spirit, spiritual truths. They will not be able to digest it. Just as a baby is not mature enough to eat adult food, spiritually impoverished people cannot feed on spiritual food. They have to be taught and fed the nutrients of the faith, very basic and elementary things.

"As a matter of fact my brothers, I could not talk to you as I talk to people who have the Spirit. I had to talk to you as though you belonged to this world, as children in the Christian faith. I had to feed you milk, not solid food, because you were not ready for it. And even now you are not ready for it, because you still live as the people of this world live." 1 Corinthians 3:1-3a

The Spirit dwells in each believer as the Temple of God, even as God's presence dwells in the Temple.

"Surely you know that you are God's temple and that God's Spirit lives in you. So if anyone destroys God's temple, God will destroy him. For God's temple is holy and you yourselves are His temple."
1 Corinthians 3:16-17

The Spirit puts us right with God, purifies us from sin, and dedicates us to God.

"Some of you were like that. But you have been purified from sin: you have been dedicated to God: you have been put right with God by the Lord Jesus Christ and by the Spirit of our God." 1 Corinthians 6:11

Paul clearly shows that the work of salvation is the work of God the Father, the work of Jesus Christ and the work of the Holy Spirit.

> "Don't you know that your body is the temple of the Holy Spirit who lives in you and who was given to you by God? You do not belong to yourselves, but to God. He bought you for a price. So use your bodies for God's glory."
> 1 Corinthians 6:19,20

Paul believes his personal opinion has the sanction of the Holy Spirit.

> "She will be happier, however, if she stays as she is. That is my opinion, and I think that I too have God's Spirit."
> 1 Corinthians 7:40

There are gifts dispensed by the Holy Spirit.

> "Now concerning what you wrote about the gifts from the Holy Spirit." 1 Corinthians 12:1

The believer has the Holy Spirit and cannot curse Jesus, and turn around in the same breath and call Him Lord.

> I want you to know that no one who is led by God's Spirit can say, "A curse on Jesus" and no one can confess 'Jesus is Lord' unless he is guided by the Holy Spirit." 1 Corinthians 12:3

The Spirit is the giver of the different gifts for the body of Christ.

> "There are different kinds of spiritual gifts, but the same Spirit gives them." 1 Corinthians 12:4

The purpose of the spiritual gifts is for the good of all, and each person has one gift or another for the benefit of all.

> "The Spirit's presence is shown in some way in each person for the good of all. The Spirit gives one person a message full of wisdom while to another person the same Spirit gives a message full of knowledge. One and the

same Spirit gives faith to one person while to another person, He gives the power to heal. The Spirit gives one person the power to work miracles: to another, the gift of speaking God's message: and to yet another, the ability to tell the difference between gifts that come from the Spirit and those that do not. To one person He gives the ability to speak in strange tongues, and to another He gives the ability to explain what is said. But it is one and the same Spirit who does all this: as He wishes, He gives a different gift to each person."
1 Corinthians 12:7-11

Paul theologized that the Spirit baptizes (submerges) us into the body of Christ to become one with Him, and also to become part of His body the Church. This same Spirit is given to us to drink; meaning God the Father and Jesus Christ our Savior give to us the Spirit to drink i.e. to live in us. This theology is complex, but that is the wonderful mystery of our God. We are baptized into Christ, and given the Spirit so that we live in Christ and the Spirit lives in us, and that means Christ lives in us because the Spirit and Christ are one. The Spirit is the Spirit of God the Father and God the Son, Jesus Christ. The simple meaning of this theology is that we are in Christ and Christ in us. We literally have our being in Him. We live and move in Him and if Christ is in us, then God the Father is in us, and we live in God because God is in Christ, and Christ is in God. (John 14:10-11, 23, Acts 17:28)

The Spirit resides in our belly i.e. In our spirits, and if the Spirit resides in our "belly" then that means health and peace to us.

> "In the same way, all of us, whether Jews or Gentiles, whether slaves or free, have been baptized into the one body by the same Spirit, and we have all been given the one Spirit to drink." 1 Corinthians 12:13

Speaking in tongues is by the power of the Holy Spirit, according to what Paul teaches the Corinthian Church. In this practice, each person speaks directly to God from his spirit by the power of the Holy Spirit.

> "The one who speaks in strange tongues does not speak to others but to God, because no one understands him. He is speaking secret truths by the power of the Spirit." 1 Corinthians 14:2

The gift of speaking in tongues is not for the building up of the church, but for the building up of the individual believer. It is definitely a gift of the Spirit, but it is not for the church, i.e. for use in the church unless it is interpreted.

> "Since you are eager to have the gifts of the Spirit, you must try above everything else to make greater use of those which help to build up the church."
> 1 Corinthians 14:12

Paul compares the Spiritual nature of Christ to the physical nature of Adam, in explaining the resurrection. Here he says Christ is the life-giving Spirit. Spirit here, I believe, is referring both to the Spiritual nature of Christ and to the Spirit Himself who is one with Christ.

> "The first man, Adam, was created a living being, but the last Adam is the life-giving Spirit. It is not the Spiritual that comes first, but the physical, and then the Spiritual."
> 1 Corinthians 15:45b-46

Questions

1. How did Paul win so many souls for Christ and establish so many churches in a Gentile culture?
   1 Corinthians 2:3-5; Galatians 1:11-23; 3:1-5; 4:6;
   Ephesians 1:11-13; 1 Thessalonians 1:5-8; 4:8
2. How does God reveal Himself to us? 1 Corinthians 2:9-12
3. How does the believer receive the mind of Christ? Why is it extremely important that you have and live with the mind of Christ daily? 1 Corinthians 2:13-16; 3:1-3
4. Do you treat your body as the temple of the Holy Spirit? 1 Corinthians 3:16-23; 6:8-20; 9:24-27;
   2 Corinthians 3:16-18; 6:14-18
5. What gifts does the Holy Spirit have for the true believer and for what purpose? 1 Corinthians 12-14
   (See especially 1 Corinthians 12:7-11)
6. What do you know about baptism in the Holy Spirit and speaking in tongues? Is it of the Holy Spirit or of Satan? Is it relevant for today's Christians? Acts 2:1-4;   1 Corinthians 14:1-33
7. Why did tongues cause so much confusion in the Corinthian church? 1 Corinthians 12; 14:1-20
8. Why did Christ, the Son of the Living God, have to become the Son of Man in order to save us? Matthew 16:16; 1 Corinthians 15:45-58

THE BOOK OF II CORINTHIANS

The Spirit, Paul propounds, is a gift from God to us, to guarantee all that He has in store for us.

"It is God Himself who has set us apart, who has placed His mark of ownership upon us, and who has given us the Holy Spirit in our hearts as the guarantee of all that He has in store for us."   2 Corinthians 1:21,22

Paul talks about the reality of the Corinthian church, established by the hard work of Paul and his associates as a letter written on their hearts (Paul and his associates) written by Christ with the Spirit as the "indelible" ink.

"It is clear that Christ Himself wrote this letter, and sent it to us. It is written not with ink, but with the Spirit of the living God, and not on stone tablets but on human hearts." 2 Corinthians 3:3

The new covenant does not consist of a written law, but of the Spirit, which gives life, as opposed to the law, which brings death.

"It is He who made us capable of serving the new covenant which consists not of the written law but of the Spirit. The written law brings death, but the Spirit gives life." 2 Corinthians 3:6

Paul compares the glory of the Holy Spirit to the glory of the law, which brings death. Moses' face shone when he went up to the mountain to receive the tablets of the law, so how much more will the glory shine in our face and in us, who through faith, receive the Holy Spirit.

"If the Law, which brings death when it is in force, came with such glory, how much greater is the glory that belongs to the activity of the Spirit." 2 Corinthians 3:7d,8

Paul shows that the Spirit is "Lord" from the Old Testament. The presence of the Lord is represented by the Spirit. The Spirit who was the main force, or presence of the Lord God, The Holy One of Israel, was also referred to in the Old Testament as simply the "Lord." And wherever the Spirit is, Jesus is there also, and wherever Jesus is, God the Father is. The work of Salvation is the work of the Holy Trinity, transforming us into God's nature.

> "Now the "Lord" in this passage is the Spirit, and where the Spirit of the Lord is, there is freedom. All of us then, reflect the glory of the Lord with uncovered faces, and that same glory, coming from the Lord, who is the Spirit transforms us into His likeness in an ever greater degree of glory." 2 Corinthians 3:17,18

Note also that the Spirit liberates from whatever oppresses the believer, transforms him into His likeness "In an ever greater degree of glory", i.e. leading us into a greater degree of glory, step by step.

Again Paul emphasizes the reason for the gift of the Spirit of God, as a "guarantee that He will change our mortal bodies into immortal ones, and also as a guarantee of all that He has in store for us."

> "God is the one who has prepared us for this change; and He gave us His Spirit as the guarantee of all that He has in store for us." 2 Corinthians 5:5 (Refer also to 2 Corinthians 4:13-14)

The mark of a true servant of God is by the Holy Spirit working in him to give him purity, knowledge, patience and kindness.

> "By our purity, knowledge, patience and kindness, we have shown ourselves to be God's servants—by the Holy Spirit, by our true love." 2 Corinthians 6:6

The theology Paul propounds clearly indicates that there is only one Lord Jesus Christ and only one Spirit from God the Father, and only one God.   (See also 1 Corinthians 8:6)

> "For you gladly tolerate anyone who comes to you and preaches a different Jesus, not the one we preached; and you accept a spirit and a gospel completely different from the Spirit and the gospel you received from us!"
> 2 Corinthians 11:4

Paul blesses the Corinthian Church with the blessings of the Trinity; The Father—God, Jesus Christ the Lord, and the Holy Spirit, the presence and fellowship of God in the church and in the believer.

> "The grace of the Lord Jesus Christ, the love of God, and the fellowship of the Holy Spirit be with you all."
> 2 Corinthians 13:13

Questions

1. When does the believer receive the Holy Spirit, after repentance and baptism in water or after baptism in the Holy Spirit and fire? In other words, does a person have the Holy Spirit just because he/she does not speak in tongues? 2 Corinthians 1:21,22; Ephesians 1:13,14
2. What, according to Acts 1:8, is the purpose of the baptism in the Holy Spirit?
3. So do we need the baptism in the Holy Spirit to be saved? Galatians 4:1-7; Romans 8:1,2
4. What does the new covenant ratified by the blood of Jesus Christ consist of? 2 Corinthians 3:6-8 (By the way, what is the new covenant? Jeremiah 31:31-34; Matthew 26:26-28; John 3:3-21; 1 Corinthians 11:25; 2 Corinthians 5:17-21; Hebrews 10:11-25)
5. What does the presence of the Holy Spirit in us reminds us and makes us aware of? 2 Corinthians 3:17,18; 5:5; 6:6; Galatians 2:20; 3:13,14

THE BOOK OF GALATIANS

As the Galatians continue to live in "doubt and unbelief", Paul had to challenge them to find out for themselves, whether God gave His Spirit to them because they were obedient to the Mosaic Law or whether through faith in Christ Jesus. The answer, of course, is that we receive the Spirit through faith, not through obedience to the law. Paul emphasizes that the Christian life is begun by God's Spirit and must end by God's Spirit. And miracles are the work of God's Spirit.

> "Tell me this one thing; did you receive God's Spirit by doing what the Law requires or by hearing the gospel and believing it? How can you be so foolish? You began by God's Spirit; do you now want to finish by your own power? Did all your experience mean nothing at all? Surely it meant something! Does God give you the Spirit and work miracles among you because you do what the Law requires or because you hear the gospel and believe it?" Galatians 3:2-5

Definitely the Spirit is received by faith in Jesus Christ.

> "Christ did this (see verse 13) in order that the blessing which God promised to Abraham might be given to the Gentiles by means of Jesus Christ, so that through faith we might receive the Spirit promised by God."
> Galatians 3:13,14

The Spirit is given to the believer as a proof that he has become God's son (child).

> "To show that you are His sons, God sent the Spirit of His Son into our hearts, the Spirit who cries out, 'Father my Father'. So then, you are no longer a slave but a son. Since you are His sons, God will give you all that He has for His sons." Galatians 4:6,7

In comparing the law and grace, Paul uses the two sons of Abraham, one born to Sarah and the other to Hagar. Those under the old covenant are in slavery to the law, but those who through faith are born of the Spirit are free.

> "At that time the son who was born in the usual way persecuted the one who was born because of God's Spirit, and it is the same now." Galatians 4:29

Arguing against being subjected to the law is Paul's main point. The law enslaves, faith sets free, or appropriately, by faith through grace we can look forward to a union with God on earth here and eternally through the power of the Spirit already given to us to guarantee this very union. We who have the Spirit can hope for this union, but those without the Spirit cannot confidently say so.

> "As for us, our hope is that God will put us right with Him; and this is what we wait for, by the power of God's Spirit, working through our faith." Galatians 5:5

Paul belabors the point everywhere in his letters that the believer receives the Spirit as a gift from God, indicating that such a person has become a child of God. Now the believer must submit His will to the Spirit. Such a person must let the Spirit be the Lord of his life. If this happens, he will gain total control over the flesh, or his lower human nature, which desires to engage in such sinful lifestyles as fornication, drunkenness, immorality, hatred, anger, etc. Instead of these, he will be filled with the fruit of the Spirit which is the nature of God—Love, Peace, Joy, Mercy, etc. The Spirit also frees us from the demands of the law, and eliminates unnecessary opposition within our inner self— and our physical nature.

> "What I say is this, let the Spirit direct your lives, and you will not satisfy the demands of the human nature. For what our human nature wants is opposed to what the Spirit wants. And what the Spirit wants is opposed to what our human nature wants. These two are enemies and this

means that you cannot do what you want to do. If the Spirit leads you then you are not subject to the Law. What human nature does is quite plain."
Galatians 5:16-19

The purpose of the Spirit is to give life, and the fruit of true life is Love, Peace, Joy, Faith, Hope, and eternal life.
"But the Spirit produces love, joy, peace, patience, kindness, goodness, faithfulness, humility, and self-control. There is no law against such things as these. And those who belong to Christ Jesus have put to death their human nature with all its passions and desires. The Spirit has given us life, He must also control our lives." Galatians 5:22-25

Paul concludes Galatians by reminding his readers that there are two kinds of life—life in the flesh and life in the Spirit; and each is compared to a seed. If they plant the seed of the flesh, they will reap the fruit of the flesh, which will be death. If they plant the seed of the Spirit, they will reap life, which is the fruit of the Spirit.

Life in the Spirit includes loving and forgiving one another, carrying one another's burdens, giving to the poor and needy, etc. Life in the flesh also involves selfishness, greed, etc. Each will produce according to its kind. You will reap what you sow.
"But do not deceive yourselves; no one makes a fool of God. A person will reap exactly what he plants, if he plants in the field of his natural desires, from it he will gather the harvest of death; if he plants in the field of the Spirit, from the Spirit he will gather the harvest of eternal life." Galatians 6:7,8

Questions

1. What qualifies you as a candidate for the Holy Spirit to dwell in you? (not upon you i.e. baptism into the Spirit) Galatians 3:2-5; 13; 14; John 7:37-39
2. Who are you in Christ Jesus and whose are you? Galatians 4:6, 29; Romans 8:14-17; 2 Corinthians 5:17-21
3. Are you living a life controlled by your flesh or by the Holy Spirit? Galatians 5:5-7; 13-26
4. Are you living under the Law or under grace? Galatians 6:7-8; 13-16; Ephesians 2:1-10; Hebrews 4:14-16
5. What is redemption? Leviticus 25:25-48; Ruth 2-4; Isaiah 53; Philippians 2:1-16
6. Have you been redeemed? Isaiah 43:1-3; Galatians 3:13,14

THE BOOK OF EPHESIANS

The Spirit is God's approval that we are His children, and it is also a guarantee of what God has promised us, namely— freedom from oppression and the gift of eternal life.

> "You believed in Christ, and God put His stamp of ownership on you by giving you the Holy Spirit He had promised. The Spirit is the guarantee that we shall receive what God has promised His people, and this assures us that God will give complete freedom to those who are His. Let us praise His glory." Ephesians 1:13c-14

The Spirit is the giver of wisdom; He reveals God to us; He is the revelation knowledge of God. He enlightens the believer, i.e. renews his mind, transforms his spirit, and gives him understanding. He is the power at work in us to witness, by word and deed, of the love and liberating power of God from sin, sickness, disease and death. It was through the power of the Spirit that Jesus was raised from the dead. He is the mighty power of God able to do all things and nothing is impossible unto Him. This power is ours through faith in Jesus Christ.

By the power of the Holy Spirit we too can rule with Christ over all heavenly rulers, authorities and powers and lords, in this world and in the hereafter as believers, and it is guaranteed to us through the gift of the Holy Spirit.

> "I remember you in my prayers and ask the God of our Lord Jesus Christ, the glorious Father, to give you the Spirit, who will make you wise and reveal God to you, so that you will know Him. I ask that your minds may be opened to see His light, so that you will know what is the hope to which He has called you, how rich are the wonderful blessings He promises His people, and how very great is His power at work in us who believe. This power working in us is the same as the mighty strength, which He

used when He raised Christ from death and seated Him at His right side in the heavenly world. Christ rules there above all heavenly rulers, authorities, powers, and lords: He has a title superior to all titles of authority in this world and in the next." Ephesians 1:16b-21; 2:6

There is only one Spirit through whom all believers, both Jews and Gentiles, come to the presence of the Father.

"It is through Christ that all of us, Jews and Gentiles, are able to come in the one Spirit into the presence of the Father." Ephesians 2:18

It is through the Spirit that all believers are built together as one body, into God's temple.

"In union with Him, you too are being built together with all the others into a place where God lives through His Spirit." Ephesians 2:22

Revelation of God's hidden truth is through the Holy Spirit.

"In the past mankind was not told this secret, but God has revealed it now by the Spirit to His Holy apostles and prophets." Ephesians 3:5

The Spirit supplies spiritual strength, inner strength for our needs. He fills us with Christ, so He can make His home in our hearts. Through faith He establishes us in love, making us strong and firm in love. He gives us understanding of the breath, width, length and depth of Christ's love. He makes us like unto God; giving us and filling us with God's own nature.
(2 Corinthians 5:17-21)

"I ask God from the wealth of His glory to give you power through His Spirit, to be strong in your inner selves, and I pray that Christ will make His home in your hearts through faith. I pray that you may have your roots and foundation in love, so that you together with all God's people may have the power to understand how broad, and long, how high and deep is Christ's love. Yes, may you come to know His love, although it can never be fully known – and so be completely filled with the very nature of God." Ephesians 3:16-19

The Holy Spirit of God gives the peace and the unity that should bind us together in Christ as one body.

"Show your love by being tolerant of one another. Do your best to preserve the unity which the Spirit gives by means of the peace that binds you together. There is one body, and one Spirit just as there is one hope to which God has called you. There is one Lord, one faith, one baptism, there is one God and Father of all mankind, who is Lord of all, works through all and is in all".
Ephesians 4:2c-6

We can make God's Holy Spirit sad by not living in love and forgiveness, but rather hating each other, and being filled with evil passions, bitterness and anger. For He is God's mark of ownership and guarantee that on the Day of the Lord we will be set free.

"And do not make God's Holy Spirit sad; for the Spirit is God's mark of ownership on you, a guarantee that the day will come when God will set you free."
Ephesians 4:30

We must let the Spirit fill us or be drunk with the Spirit.

"Do not get drunk with wine, which will only ruin you; instead be filled with the Spirit." Ephesians 5:18

The Word of God is a sword given to us by the Spirit to fight the enemy (The enemy is Satan and his cohorts).

"And accept salvation as a helmet, and the word of God as a sword which the Spirit gives you." Ephesians 6:17

We should pray as the Spirit leads us and inspires us.

"Pray on every occasion as the Spirit leads."
Ephesians 6:18c

Questions

1. Did you receive the Holy Spirit when you believed, repented of your sins and were baptized in water in the name of Jesus? Ephesians 1:13,14;
   Galatians 3:1-5; 13,14; 5:16-25; John 7:37-39
2. What then is the difference between being filled with the Holy Spirit and baptism with the Holy Spirit and fire? Matthew 10:1; Mark 6:7-13; 16:15-18; Luke 9:1,2;
   Acts 1:8; Romans 8:1-17; 1 Thessalonians 1:5-8
3. According to scriptures, we can grieve the Holy Spirit. What are some of the things we do to grieve the Holy Spirit? Ephesians 4:30; 5:18; 1 Corinthians 10:1-13;
   1 Thessalonians 5:14-28
4. What weapons does the Spirit give us or admonish us to wear to be able to stand firm against Satan and defeat him? Ephesians 6:10-20; 2 Corinthians 10:3-6

THE BOOK OF PHILIPPIANS

The Holy Spirit is the Spirit of Jesus Christ and He the spirit sets us free from all spiritual and temporal bondages.

> "And I will continue to be happy, because I know that by means of your prayers and the help which comes from the Spirit of Jesus Christ, I shall be set free."
> Philippians 1:18b-19

We must have fellowship with the Spirit at all times as believers.

> "You have fellowship with the Spirit, and you have kindness and compassion for one another."
> Philippians 2:1c

Even our worship cannot be effective if it is not accomplished by means of God's Spirit. It is only effective if we do it by the aid of the Holy Spirit.

> "It is we, not they, who have received the true circumcision. For we worship God by means of His Spirit, and rejoice in our life in union with Christ Jesus. We do not put any trust in external ceremonies." Philippians 3:3

Questions

1. Now that you know quite a bit about who the Spirit is and what He has given you, what role is He supposed to play in your life to bring you to your God-appointed destination? Philippians 1:18-19; 2:1-16; 3:3-4
2. Is it possible that we can do things and act in such a way as to prevent and obstruct the Holy Spirit from accomplishing His plan for us? Philippians 2:1; Ephesians 4:30; 5:18; 1 Thessalonians 5:19-21

The Spirit gives love to the believer, and the faithful servants of God.

> "He has told us of the love that the Spirit has given you."
> Colossians 1:8

The Spirit is the giver of knowledge, wisdom, and understanding. The Spirit reveals the knowledge of God's will.

> "We ask God to fill you with the knowledge of His will, with all the wisdom and understanding that His Spirit gives."
> Colossians 1:9b

Questions

1. What specific gift(s) does the Holy Spirit give to us to make it easier for us to cooperate with Him to accomplish His purpose in us? Colossians 1:8, 9
2. How are we supposed to pray for ourselves and others to keep the Spirit working in us and through us? Colossians 1:9-21

THE BOOKS OF I AND II THESSALONIANS

The Good News must be preached with the manifestations and evidence of the power of the Holy Spirit.

> "For we brought the Good News to you, not with words only but also with power and the Holy Spirit and with complete conviction of its truth." 1 Thessalonians 1:5

True joy comes from the Holy Spirit and is given to those who embrace the Good News.

The Holy Spirit enabled the gentiles to receive the message with joy in spite of persecution.

> "You imitated us and the Lord, and even though you suffered much, you received the message with the joy that comes from the Holy Spirit." 1 Thessalonians 1:6

Whoever rejects God's message, rejects also God and His Spirit.

> "So then, whoever rejects this teaching is not rejecting man, but God, who gives you His Holy Spirit."
> 1 Thessalonians 4:8

The believer can restrain the Holy Spirit by living in sin, despising inspired preaching or messages, and by not putting all things to the test by the power of the Holy Spirit.

> "Do not restrain the Holy Spirit, do not despise inspired messages, put all things to the test. Keep what is good; and avoid every kind of evil." 1 Thessalonians 5:19-22

We are saved by the Spirit's power in order that we might be made God's holy people through our faith in the truth.

> "For God chose you as the first to be saved by the Spirit's power to make you His holy people and by your faith in the truth." 2 Thessalonians 2:13c

Questions

1. How do we grow and build the church of God, both numerically and spiritually? 1 Thessalonians 1:5
2. If we want to live a life of victory and joy in a hopeless, powerless, and helpless world, who should help us in this endeavor? 1 Thessalonians 1:5-10; 2 Thessalonians 2:13

THE BOOKS OF I AND II TIMOTHY

The Holy Spirit approved of Christ and witnessed that He was truly the right person the Son of God and the Son of Man.

> "He appeared in human form, was shown to be right by the Spirit." 1 Timothy 3:16b

The Spirit is the revealer of the secrets of God, of prophecy, and of things to come, a mirror through which we look into the future.

> "The Spirit says clearly that some people will abandon the faith in latter times; they will obey lying spirits and follow the teachings of demons." 1 Timothy 4:1

Paul must have placed his hands on Timothy to receive the gift of the Holy Spirit: the gift of baptism of the Holy Spirit. I personally believe that this was what happened (see Acts 19:1-7, especially verses 6 and 7). Remember, Paul chose Timothy, as his co-worker, (Acts 16:1-4) and he laid his hands on him to receive the power of the Holy Spirit (Acts 1:8) in order to be a witness of Jesus Christ. This gift is what Paul is reminding Timothy of. It is the power that fills us with love, power, authority and self-control and drives out fear. The baptism of the Holy Spirit completely drives out fear, leads us in love and authority over demonic spirits (see Luke 10:19) and self-control, righteous thinking, righteous action, righteous and victorious living.

> "For this reason I remind you to keep alive the gift that God gave you when I laid my hands on you. For the Spirit that God has given us does not make us timid, instead, His Spirit fills us with power, love and self-control."
> 2 Timothy 1:6-7

The Holy Spirit lives within our spirits – in us, and He enables or empowers us to keep the good things that have been entrusted to us.

> "Through the power of the Holy Spirit, who lives in us, keep the good things that have been entrusted to you." 2 Timothy 1:14

The word of God was inspired by the Spirit of God and is therefore necessary for our understanding of God and for our belief in what God has done and is doing. Therefore, the work of God is eternally true for all ages, for eternity. Even though the Spirit is not directly mentioned in this verse, it is implied.

> "All Scripture is inspired by God and is useful for teaching the truth, rebuking error, correcting faults, and giving instruction for right living, so that the person who serves God may be fully qualified and equipped to do every kind of good deed." 2 Timothy 3:16-17

Questions

1. How do we know for sure that Christ is who He says He is? How do we know that He is who the Word says He is? 1 Timothy 3:16; 2 Timothy 3:16,17
2. How do we know how to understand and interpret social, economic, and political events happening now, and how do we know what is about to happen in the future? 1 Timothy 4:1-3; 2 Timothy 3:1-17
3. The gifts of the Spirit, including the baptism in the Spirit, can be transferred. How is it accomplished in 2 Timothy 1:6,7? (Pastors – Does this include your ordination? Are you aware that you must be careful who lays hands on you during your ordination?)
4. How do we become faithful, diligent, dedicated, and empowered all the days of our lives as disciples of Christ? 2 Timothy 1:13,14 (Read 2 Timothy 1:13 – 2:1)
5. How do we know that the Word of God is true and that it can be trusted to do what it says? 2 Timothy 3:16,17

THE BOOK OF TITUS

God saved us through the power of the Holy Spirit, through whom we receive the New Birth, and through whom we are washed and cleansed from our sins.

The Holy Spirit is also given to us by God through Jesus, so that through Him we might receive justification and sanctification, and come to hope for eternal life, which becomes our heritage as believers.

Here we see God at work. There is a mode to God's creativity, His action, His way of doing things in the universe, His works through Jesus by the power of the Holy Spirit. That was the way creation was accomplished, that was the way our redemption was accomplished, and that is the way we are brought into fellowship with Him; and that is the way we remain in fellowship with Him, and that is the way we will achieve the resurrection and the life everlasting.

> "It was not because of any good deeds that we ourselves have done but because of His own mercy that He saved us through the Holy Spirit, who gives us new birth and new life by washing us. God poured out the Holy Spirit abundantly on us through Jesus Christ our Savior, so that by His grace we might be put right with God and come into possession of the eternal life we hope for. This is a true saying." Titus 3:5-8

Questions

Titus helps us to understand our salvation and the specific roles the Holy Spirit plays to bring this to pass. Can you identify these roles in this passage, Titus 3:3-9?

THE BOOK OF HEBREWS

The gifts of the Holy Spirit are distributed according to God's will. Miracles and wonders are also the acts of the Holy Spirit and they confirm the truth of God's word. These acts witness to the truth.

> "At the same time God added His witness to theirs by performing all kinds of miracles and wonders and by distributing the gifts of the Holy Spirit according to His will." Hebrews 2:4

The Holy Spirit was the voice that spoke through the prophets. Prophecy came from the Holy Spirit through the prophets.

> "So then, as the Holy Spirits says, If you hear God's voice today do not be stubborn as your ancestors were, when they rebelled against God, as they were that day in the desert, as they put Him to the test." Hebrews 3:7,8

Believers receive their share of the Holy Spirit by faith, together with all God's children. They should be careful not to be apostates, nor abandon their faith or become blasphemers of the Holy Spirit.

> "For how can those who abandon their faith be brought back to repent again? They were once in God's light, they tasted heaven's gift and received their share of the Holy Spirit." Hebrews 6:4

The Holy Spirit is a teacher and a revealer of the secrets or mysteries of God.

> "The Holy Spirit clearly teaches from all these arrangements that the way into the most Holy Place has not yet been opened as long as the outer tent still stands." Hebrews 9:8

The Spirit enabled Christ to offer Himself a perfect sacrifice for all humanity and for all ages.

> "Since this is true, how much more is accomplished by the blood of Christ! Through the eternal Spirit, He offered Himself as a perfect sacrifice to God. His blood will purify our consciences from useless rituals, so that we may serve the living God." Hebrews 9:14

Through the Spirit, who is eternal, Christ offered Himself for all humanity; Christ could not and would not have died for us without the power and efficacy of the Holy Spirit. Throughout all of the Scriptures, God's word is clear; that the work of Salvation is the work of God, meaning the work of God, the Father, the Son and the Holy Spirit. The Holy Spirit is a witness of the things of God, through the scriptures, through miracles and wonders.

> "And the Holy Spirit also gives us His witness. First He says, 'This is the covenant that I will make with them in the days to come' says the Lord. 'I will put my laws in their hearts, and write them on their minds.' And then He says, 'I will not remember their sins and evil deeds any longer.'" Hebrews 10:15-17

The Spirit is the Spirit of grace, meaning He makes available to us the free gift of salvation; the power to break free from the bondage of sin and death, and disease. He manifests Himself through signs and miracles, and through the power and the love of God.

> "What then of the person who despises the Son of God? Who treats as cheap things the blood of God's covenant which purified him from Sin? Who insults the Spirit of grace?" Hebrews 10:29

The above is another indication that Jesus offered Himself through the Holy Spirit, and that the work of salvation is the work of God, the Father, the Son and the Holy Spirit.

Questions

1. According to the Book of Hebrews, why are the gifts of the Holy Spirit given to believers and what do they help us accomplish? Hebrews 2:4-5

2. Note carefully how the Book of Hebrews depicts the Holy Spirit. Is the Holy Spirit just a power or a "person" with power? Hebrews 3:7-15 (Beware of any teaching that says the Holy Spirit is just a "power" and not a "person", the third "person" of the Trinity.)

3. Is it possible for a true believer to turn away from the truth and denounce what he/she once believed as untruth, blaspheme God or become an apostate? How do you prevent this from happening?
   Hebrews 6:4-6; 9:8; 10:15-17; 1 John 2:26,27

The Spirit of God in us; has a "fierce desire". Is this desire driving and drawing us towards God's righteousness, God's nature? What about the grace? Grace can be interpreted to mean love and power or grace can be the free and unmerited love and mercy of God. Which one is the writer talking about, one or both? It must be both; especially love. If so, it is James contention that love is as strong as the Spirit that God places in us.

> "The Spirit that God placed in us is filled with fierce desire. But the grace that God gives is even stronger. As the scripture says, God resists the proud, but gives grace to the humble." James 4:5,6

Questions

Here is another indication of who the Holy Spirit is.
Note: Power is brute force, dynamite, explosion. If the Holy Spirit is only a force or power, how can He be full of desire and gives us grace to do and be what God has called us to do and be? Mark 16:19,20; James 4:5,6; 1 Thessalonians 1:5;
1 Peter 1:2; 11,12

THE BOOK OF 1 PETER

The Spirit makes us a Holy people, set us apart for God and by God, to obey Jesus Christ our Savior, and to be purified by His blood, and to be filled with all heavenly blessings.

"You were chosen according to the purposes of God the Father and were made a holy people by His Spirit, to obey Jesus Christ, and be purified by His blood. May grace and peace be yours in full measure." 1 Peter 1:2

The Spirit through the prophets of old revealed the things which were to be fulfilled about Jesus, in our age; and the same Spirit gave ability, power to people who carried the Good News to those whom God has chosen to be saved.

"This was the time to which Christ Spirit in them was pointing in predicting the suffering that Christ would have to endure and the glory that would follow. God revealed to these prophets that their work was not for their own benefit, but for yours as they spoke about those things which you have now heard from the messengers who announced the Good News by the power of the Holy Spirit sent from heaven. These are things which even the angels would like to understand."
1 Peter 1:11,12

The Believer must willingly endure suffering and persecution with the knowledge that the Spirit of God is resting on him. It Is also an indication that the world does not approve of us.

"Happy are you if you are insulted because you are Christ's followers; this means that the glorious Spirit, the Spirit of God, is resting on you. " 1 Peter 4:14

All scripture is inspired by the Holy Spirit and it is eternally true see also 2 Timothy 3:16-17

"Above all else, however, remember that no one can explain by himself or herself a prophecy in the Scriptures. For no prophetic message ever came just from human will, but people were under the control of the Holy Spirit as they spoke the message that came from God."
2 Peter 1:20-21

Questions

1. According to Peter, what is the purpose of suffering for Christians? How does the Holy Spirit help us endure suffering and persecution? I Peter 1:11,12, 4:13,14
2. How does God let us know that His Word is eternally true? 2 Peter 1:20,21; 2 Timothy 3:16,17

THE BOOK OF 1 JOHN

The Holy Spirit is poured on us by Jesus Christ to help us understand His truth.

"But you had the Holy Spirit poured out on you by Christ, and so all of you know the truth." 1 John 2:20

Obedience to the Spirit is essential if we are going to keep growing in the truth imparted to us by Him.

"I am writing this to you about those who are trying to deceive you. But as for you, Christ had poured out His Spirit on you. As long as His Spirit remains in you, you do not need anyone to teach you. For His Spirit teaches you about everything, and what He teaches is true, not false. Obey the Spirit's teaching then, and remain in union with Christ." 1 John 2:26,27

The gift of the Spirit to us confirms that God lives in us.

"Whoever obeys God's commands lives in union with God and God lives in union with him. And because of the Spirit that God has given us, we know that God lives in union with us." 1 John 3:24

We are not to believe all who claim to have the Spirit, but to test what they have, for not all who claim to have the Spirit have the Spirit that comes from God. False prophets, who claim that Jesus is not both human and divine, have Satan's spirit.

"My dear friends do not believe all who claim to have the Spirit, but test them to see if the spirit they have comes from God. For many false prophets have gone out everywhere. This is how you will be able to know whether it is God's Spirit; anyone who acknowledges that Jesus Christ came as a human being, has the Spirit who came from God. But anyone who denies this about Jesus does not have the Spirit from God. The spirit that he has is from

the Enemy of Christ. You heard that it would come, and now it is here in the world already."
1 John 4:1-5

Another way by which we can clearly demonstrate that we have God's Spirit is to overcome the world, because God's Spirit is more powerful than the spirit of Satan who is in the world.

"But you belong to God my children, and have defeated the false prophets. Because the Spirit who is in you, is more powerful than the spirit in those who belong to the world." 1 John 4:4

Another way we can tell the difference between the false prophets and true believers is that the false prophets will not listen to the truth, but the believer who has God's Spirit will listen and obey the truth.

"Whoever knows God listens to us; whoever does not belong to God does not listen to us. This then is how we can tell the difference between the Spirit of truth and the spirit of error." 1 John 4:6

Again St John declares that the gift of God's Spirit to us is a manifestation that God has given Himself to us, and that He is living in us.

"We are sure that we live in union with God, and that He lives in union with us, because He has given us His Spirit."
1 John 4:13

The Spirit testifies to the redemptive work of Christ symbolized by the water and the blood; forgiveness of sins, and substitution of life for life because it is the Spirit of truth. The Spirit is truth personified; so His testimony is eternally true.

These three mentioned above also witness to the redemptive work of Christ, namely the water, the blood and the Spirit. All three are vital to the redemption and reconciliation of man

(humanity) to God. Man's redemption couldn't take place without these three in operation.

Man (descendants of Adam) does not only need redemption from his predicament, he needs forgiveness through the washing and cleansing of his sins; he also needs reconciliation to God and renewal of his spirit, and this is accomplished by the gift of God's Spirit to our spirit.

> "Jesus Christ is the one who came with the water of His baptism, and the blood of His death. He came not only with the water, but with both the water and the blood. And the Spirit Himself testifies that this is true, because the Spirit is truth. There are three witnesses, the Spirit, the water and the blood, and all three give the same testimony." 1 John 5:6-8

Questions

1. According to John, why is the Holy Spirit poured out on us, the believers? 1 John 2:20,26,27; 3:24; 4:13
2. How do we know the difference between true prophets and false prophets? 1 John 4:1-8
3. How does the true believer overcome the world? 1 John 4:4

THE BOOK OF JUDE

Those who do not have the Holy Spirit cause divisions in the body of Christ, they live according to their natural desires and inclination, they lust after the flesh, and they have a selfish and greedy goal in life.

> "These are the people who cause divisions, who are controlled by their natural desires, who do not have the Spirit." Jude 1:19

Those who have the Spirit however build themselves up in faith and pray in the power of the Spirit.

> "But you my friends keep on building yourselves up on your most sacred faith. Pray in the power of the Holy Spirit, and keep yourselves in the Love of God as you wait for our Lord Jesus Christ in His mercy to give you eternal life." Jude 1:20-21

Questions

According to Jude, how do we tell the true believer from the false one? Where do you honestly see yourself? What do you have to do to change your stance, if your lifestyle does not fit the Biblical model? Jude 1:19-21

THE BOOK OF REVELATION

John received God's Revelation given to Christ "in order to show what must happen soon", (Revelation 1:1) through the power of the Spirit who took control of John.

> "On the Lord's Day the Spirit took control of me, and I heard a loud voice that sounded like a trumpet, speaking behind me." Revelation 1:10

The work of God, after the resurrection of Jesus Christ, is done by the Spirit. He is the one who "speaks" to the churches through the messengers.

> "If you have ears, then listen to what the Spirit says to the churches. "To those who win the victory I will give the right to eat the fruit of the Tree of Life that grows in the Garden of God." (Revelation 2:7) "If you have ears then listen to what the Spirit says to the churches. "Those who win the victory will not be hurt by the second death." (Revelation 2:11) "If you have ears then listen to what the Spirit says to the churches. "To those who win the victory I will give some of the hidden manna. I will also give each of them a white stone on which is written a new name that no one knows except the one who receives it." Revelation 2:11-17

Jesus speaks to the church but He speaks to us through the power of the Holy Spirit.

> "If you have ears then listen to what the Spirit says to the churches." Revelation 2:29
> "If you have ears then listen to what the Spirit says to the churches." Revelation 3:6
> "If you have ears then listen to what the Spirit says to the churches." Revelation 3:13
> "If you have ears then listen to what the Spirit says to the churches." Revelation 3:22

Through the power and the operations of the Spirit, John was able to look into heaven and to see the throne of God.

> "At once the Spirit took control of me. There in heaven was a throne with someone sitting on it." Revelation 4:3

I have no idea what this means, but this is what some commentaries have to say. The "seven spirits" is another name for the Holy Spirit. See also Zachariah 4:2-6 where the seven lambs are equated with the one spirit.

I have no idea what this means, but this is what some commentaries have to say. "The horns symbolize strength and power. (See 1 Kings 22:11 and Zachariah 1:18) Although Christ is the sacrificial lamb, He is no way weak. He was killed but now he lives in God's strength and power. (Zachariah 4:2-10) The eyes are equated with the seven lamps and one Spirit." (See Revelation 5:6)

The Holy Spirit can give us power to do anything God wants us to do. He can give us power to proclaim God's word in such a form and fashion that will convict sinners of their sins; power to heal the sick or raise the dead, power to make the impossible, possible. Revelation 11:4-6, Luke 10:19,
Matthew 10:1-15

The Spirit is a witness to the work and word of God. He confirms and affirms what we read in God's word, by saying to our spirits, yes it is true, yes it is believable, yes it is faithful, yes, you can depend on it. He puts His stamp of approval on what we read. He gives us a Revelation of what we read in such a vivid fashion that we believe it in total, and that amounts to faith. We not only hear the word, but we know the word, we not only hear, but we see the word in vivid and clear pictures, like a television. Not only do they announce the news, they show it, and you can see it for yourself. These two things make it believable.

It is necessary that we read God's word daily, so the Holy Spirit can witness to the truth of God's word by giving us the Revelation (television picture) of God's word.

> "Then I heard a voice from heaven saying, 'Write this, Happy are those who from now on die in the service of the Lord.' 'Yes indeed', answered the Spirit. 'They will rest from their hard work, because the result of their work goes with them.'" Revelation 14:13

By the power of the Holy Spirit John is transported to a desert Island. Here we see it was an Angel who carried him; but the Holy Spirit prepared John and made him transportable. The Angel was only doing what he was told to do as God's holy minister.

> "The Spirit took control of me, and the Angel carried me to a desert. There I saw a woman sitting on a red beast that had names insulting to God written all over it. The beast had seven heads and ten horns." Revelation 17:3

This was a similar instance from the last Revelation 17:3

> "One of the Seven Angels who had the seven bowls full of the seven last plagues, came to me and said, 'Come and I will show you the Bride, the wife of the Lamb.' The Spirit took control of me and the Angel carried me to the top of a very high mountain." Revelation 21:9-10

The Spirit is of God and comes from God, and He is given to all the prophets, and of course, to all believers for the salvation of God's people.

> "Then the Angel said to me, 'These words are true and can be trusted'. And the Lord God who gives His Spirit to the prophets has sent His Angel to show His servants what must happen very soon." Rev 22::6

Even if the Spirit does not give us a "television" picture of God's word, we must still believe it as true, as we would believe the radio announcer, who is not able to give us a television picture of the news.

The best way to believe is to be a hearer and a doer of the Word (John 20:27-29; James 1:21-25; Romans 10:17). The second best way is to be a hearer and a seer
(Revelation 1:9-20; 22:7-17). The tragedy is many believers act like Thomas. They want to "see" before they believe. Such a person will never be blessed by receiving an answer to his/her prayers whether it be for healing or any kind of request
(Mark 11:20-24). Miracles happen when we believe because we heard (Mark 5:24-34; John 11:40). The Holy Spirit will work with all believers – the true church, and when the time comes for Jesus, the Lamb, to be revealed, both (the Spirit and the Church – The Bride) will agree on His coming, we will see Him face to face and will welcome Him with open arms because we heard and believed.

> "I, Jesus, have sent my Angel to announce these things to you in the churches. I am descended from the family of David; I am the bright morning star. The Spirit and the Bride say come." Revelation 22:16-17

Everyone who hears this must also say "come". (The witness of John). Revelation 22:17b

Questions

1. Why did John receive the revelation given to him by Jesus Christ? Revelation 1:1-10

2. How is the doctrine of the Trinity portrayed in Revelations, especially at the beginning?
   Revelation 2:11; 17,29; 3:18; 13:22; Acts 2:32-34
   (Note: Jesus is not the same as the Holy Spirit, or vice-versa. The Holy Spirit proceeds from the Father and the Son. The Holy Spirit is the Spirit of both the Father and the Son. There is only one Spirit between Father and Son.)
   Jesus Christ lives in the Father and the Father lives in the Son (Jesus Christ). John 14:5-31. GOD WANTS TO LIVE IN US THROUGH JESUS CHRIST WHO LIVES IN US, THROUGH THE OPERATION OF THE HOLY SPIRIT WHO ALSO LIVES IN US. John 15:1-10. WE MUST STUDY THIS TRUTH, BELIEVE IT, AND LIVE IT.

3. Have you ever had dreams, visions, and revelation knowledge from the Holy Spirit?
   Revelation 17:3; 21:9-10; 22:6
   The gifts of the Holy Spirit are not reserved for a few "holy" and "privileged" Christians, it is for us all who diligently seek and ask for it. Matthew 7:7; John 7:37-39; Acts 2:37-39

4. If we have the Holy Spirit, who is our Helper, Comforter, Teacher, Counselor, Constant Companion, and our empowerment, why do we need angels to help us?
   Hebrews 1:1-14

How To Redefine The Subject Of The Holy Spirit

1. Go through the Bible and recheck on the passages from the RSV or KJV.
2. Read some good books and commentaries on the subject and refine our headings and topics for each verse.
3. Define words and phrases that refer or talk about the Spirit.
4. Check every cross Biblical reference.

NOTES

NOTES

NOTES

NOTES

NOTES

Testimonials

I have known Dr. Lartey as a teacher and minister of the Word for over 25 years. I was blessed to be part of his class on The Holy Spirit at Hamilton Park UMC in the mid 1980's

Dr. Lartey's God-Given gift as an expository teacher comes shining forth in this book.
<u>The Holy Spirit in the New Testament</u>, details the meaning of the scripture concerning the person, power, and presence of the Holy Spirit. I am honored to have been used to help Dr. Lartey prepare the manuscript for this book.

Glinda Shaffer
McKinney, Texas

My wife, Alison, and I first met Dr. Kwame Lartey as a minister of the Word at Hamilton Park UMC in 1989. I recall being immediately impressed by his deep understanding of scripture and his sincere care and concern for our young family. As I read the text in preparing editing notes for updates to <u>The Holy Spirit in the New Testament</u>, I realized that I was receiving a profound understanding of the dynamic power of the Holy Spirit! The commentary is transformational as you allow the person, power, and presence of the Holy Spirit to touch your heart.

Ron T. Brown
Allen, Texas

I've had the awesome privilege of being a part of Dr. Lartey's early-morning prayer line since December 2016. It's through this ministry that I've come to appreciate the breadth and depth of his Spirit-given gifts and oh how he has impacted my life with those mighty tools. Meeting Dr. Lartey was a pivotal moment in my life, one which has been the springboard for a revitalized love for God and His work for me.

While helping add text to <u>The Holy Spirit in the New Testament</u>, I was again amazed at Dr. Lartey's mastery of the subject and challenged spiritually by the content. What a gift we have in the Holy Spirit. Thank You Lord for speaking through Your worthy vessel in such a mighty way.

Roderick D. Sample
Rowlett, TX

It was October 1988, when my darling wife Shirley, approached me with good news. We were pregnant! Being members of the Hamilton Park UMC, we were members of a Friday Night Bible Study that eventually turned into a Friday Night Prayer Session. Rev. Kwame Lartey and his wife Robbie were the facilitators. We have now known Dr. Lartey, for about 33 years. During these studies, Dr. Lartey was teaching us the study of the Holy Spirit, and how to pray in the Spirit. We would pray for hours for our local churches, the members, our families and personal needs, the nation and the world, and we also prayed for conception for young couples who were having problems with fertility issues.

The Holy Spirit had given Dr. Lartey the vision and revelation knowledge about families. He first prayed for Vince and Zina Crawford and they had conceived each year for about 5 years successfully. During one of the sessions Shirley had asked for prayer to conceive, and Dr. Lartey and the group prayed for her by the laying on of hands, and so she conceived, but the baby died in the womb after 7 months of conception. Dr. Lartey called us in again, and under his direction the whole group prayed for us again. So, we were very excited about this pregnancy. We had learned that we were having twins, and this great news had us both very excited and nervous. The group continued to support us and undergird us with their prayers and intercession, and we constantly placed our pregnancy on the Throne of Grace. Shortly after Shirley had conceived she had a special sonogram appointment and the OB/GYN Doctor had explained to us, that a maternity leave would need to begin due to Shirley's blood flow condition; therefore, she was placed on home bed rest. Also, during this time the Doctor suggested that we have an Amino Synthesis (the set of biochemical processes by which the various amino acids are produced from other compounds; the building blocks for proteins and more) which we declined. Instead we fell to our knees, prayed and believed that we would have two healthy sons, through God's grace!

Soon, Shirley was admitted into the hospital. Her blood flow condition was not getting any better and the only movement our Doctor wanted was for her to go from the bed to the bathroom. She was there at Baylor (Dallas) hospital for seven (7) weeks, and on Sunday, April 23, 1989, around 12:30 PM, Remington's heart rate went down, for about 15 seconds.

Then around 12:45 PM, Russell's heart rate went down for about 15 seconds. The resident on duty phoned our Doctor to report the situation with the twins heart rate and he arrived around 2:00 PM. After examining my wife, he announced that we would be having babies that evening, and on April 23, 1989, Remington Leif Bouyer was born at 4:04 PM, followed by Russell Lance Bouyer at 4:06 PM via a cesarean section; and even though several neonatal specialists were in the delivery room; God had this situation in hand and under control by His Grace and mercy, so they were not needed. Dr. Kwame Lartey was there for us the whole time, praying and teaching us how to stand on God's Word and His promises. The Bible says, "where two or three are gathered in His name He is in the midst," and to this day, the twins are now, 29 years of age; through God's FAVOR, and we thank God and Dr. Lartey for his love, support and prayers!!!

Roger & Shirley Bouyer
Frisco, TX
Hamilton Park UMC

In 1987 I met Dr. Kwame Lartey the Associate Pastor of Hamilton Park United Methodist Church. He was the Leader of the Bible Study and Prayer Class, and he was teaching on the Power of the Holy Spirit and Prayer.

In this class I gained the real understanding of the Triune, "God the Father, God the Son and God the Holy Spirit" and the Prayer Jesus taught the Disciples. As I grew in my understanding of the Word of God, my prayers became real, my Faith in God grew, and I began to feel the presence of the

Holy Spirit in my life, leading me in the path of righteousness as a believer of Jesus Christ.

Over these years I have experienced the manifestation of the Holy Spirit as I began to live the nine Fruits of the Spirit in Galatians 5: 22 " Love, Joy, Peace, Patience, Kindness, Goodness, Faithfulness, Gentleness and Self-Control, which have really blessed my life.

Dr. Lartey's teaching is still impacting my life today. In 1995 I was obedient to the Holy Spirit's voice and accepted my Call to Ministry where I led several Ministries and in 2009 I was appointed as an Associate Local Pastor in the same Church and is now the Prayer Minister.

It has been an amazing season in my Christian life for 31 years. I have been guided by the Holy Spirit through the Prayers, Word of Knowledge, Impartation, of my Minister, Mentor and Friend Dr. Kwame Lartey. It is always a joy hearing his scripture greeting "I am growing in Wisdom, Stature and Favor with God and Man"

I invite you the reader of this book "Victorious Living; Through the Holy Spirit" to apply the principles that he shares, because they will bless your Christian Life.

Pastor Archie C. Browne
Garland, TX
Hamilton Park UMC

It was 1986 or 1987 Dr. Lartey was excited about starting an Intercessory Prayer group at church. I had been in his Tuesday Study night Bible Study and was excited about learning more about God's words. So, when Dr. Lartey would ask me again and again about joining Intercessory Prayer I would continue to give a firm no!

Dr. Lartey never gave up on me and he didn't wear me down either. The Holy Spirit guided me and gave me the desire to seek God in even a deeper way. Those nights he would teach us the deep things of God and we would see miracles happen in our lives and the life of the church. Dr. Lartey would teach on the Holy Spirit and that the Holy Spirit wasn't just for pastors, but the Holy Spirit wanted a relationship with us. I finally realized the Holy Spirit wanted me to have a relationship with Him and so, I received the baptism of the Holy Spirit and my Spiritual life changed me. I discovered the Holy Spirit cares about my everyday needs and cares. I discovered the Holy Spirit obeys God and will never lead me astray from God. This is what Dr. Lartey taught each Friday night with such audacious passion the word of God through the scripture. So, if you are looking for some good ideas on Spirituality this might not be the book for you. If you are seeking God and want to go through scripture with prayer and allow the Holy Spirit to teach you, then you will be enriched by God's word though scripture.

Studying under Dr. Lartey has encouraged me, like him, I am growing in wisdom and in stature and in favor with God and man. (Luke 2:52).

Beverly L Galimore
Dallas, TX
Hamilton Park UMC

TOTM. My first understanding of the Holy Spirit came about during Sunday School class taught by Rev. Lartey during the mid-80s at Hamilton Park UMC. I was introduced to the book by Benny Hinn (Good Morning Holy Spirit) and various TV ministers through Kenneth Copeland. I had a desire to speak in tongues, which came during one of my visits with Rev. Lartey in the Harambe House. God does give us the desires of our hearts. Over the last 30+ years, my gift has been undergirded through my participation in the Prayer Ministry at Hamilton Park.

The Holy Spirit has been my constant Companion and my strength, my hope and my comfort during my ordeal with health issues; dealing with my heart, bleeding from unknown areas and unexplained weight loss (according to John 14:15-17 "If ye love me, keep my commandments. And I will pray the Father, and he shall give you another Comforter, that he may abide with you forever; even the Spirit of truth; whom the world cannot receive, because it seeth him not, neither knoweth him; but you know him, for he dwelleth with you, and shall be in you). It appears I was given a "thorn in the flesh", however, because I had the hook up with the Holy Spirit, I was able to go through this health ordeal. So, this book will help you find the same guidance, direction, comfort, strength and constant companionship I have received. Praise God!!!

V. Reginald Hopkins, CPA
Mesquite, TX
Hamilton Park UMC

I thank God for knowing Rev. Dr. Kwame O. Lartey for over 30 years. My family and I were members of his church in Wichita Falls, TX. I taught Sunday school, was an usher, sung in the choir, and attended Bible study and Intercessory Prayer every Friday night, and many more.

One night I had a dream, the Lord spoke to me out of scripture. First, through 2 Timothy 2:15 (Study to show thyself approved unto God). Second, through James 2:14-16 (What doth it profit, my brethren, though a man say he hath faith, and have not works? Can faith save him? If a brother or sister be naked, and destitute of daily food, and one of you say unto them, depart in peace, be ye warmed and filled; notwithstanding ye give them not those things which are needful to the body; what doth it profit? Even so, faith, if it hath not works, is dead, being alone. Yea, a man may say Thou hast faith, and I have works; shew me thy faith without thy works, and I will shew thee my faith by my works. Thou believe that there is one God; thou does well; the devils also believe, and tremble. But wilt thou know, O vain man, that faith without works is dead? Was not Abraham our father justified by works, when he had offered Isaac his son upon the altar? Seeth thou how faith wrought with his works, and by works was faith made perfect? And the scripture was fulfilled which saith, ABRAHAM BELIEVED GOD, AND IT WAS IMPUTED UNTO HIM FOR RIGHTEOUSNESS; and he was called the Friend of God. Ye see then how that by works a man is justified, and not by faith only. Likewise, also was not Rahab the harlot justified by works, when she had received the messengers and had sent them out another way? For as the body without the spirit is dead, so faith without works is dead also.), and Third, through Matthew 6:33 (But seek ye first the kingdom of God and his righteousness and all these things shall be added unto you).

I woke up and called Rev. Lartey. He asked me to come to their home and I told him about my dream. WE prayed and asked God to give me direction and the plan for my life. After we prayed the Holy Spirit directed him to ask me, have I ever received the Baptism with the Holy Spirit and I said no. He asked me, do I want to receive it, and I said yes! (Act 19;1-7 "Paul, ask the disciples, have you received the Holy Ghost and they said, we have not so much as heard whether there be any Holy Ghost, so, he asked what then were ye baptized, and they said unto John's baptism, then Paul laid hands on them and baptized them, and the Holy Ghost came upon them).

Dr. Lartey laid his hands on me and I received the Power of the Holy Spirit. All of those who put their faith in Jesus Christ are immediately and permanently in dwelled by the Holy Spirit. The Holy Spirit helped me to understand what my spiritual gifts are, the Holy Spirit still works in me and through me as a believer to accomplish his will. His Power leads me, convicts me, teaches me and equips me to do his work and spread the gospel.

The Holy Spirit is Powerful, and the Indwelling is an Amazing gift and we should never take it lightly. I thank God for His Word in Jesus' name and I thank Rev. Lartey for his teachings.

This book Victorious Living through the Holy Spirit will do the same for you if you diligently study it and apply it.
To God Be The Glory!!!

Cathy Parker
Dallas, TX
Hamilton Park UMC